KENTUCKY
Sweet & Savory

Finding the Artisan Foods and Beverages of the Bluegrass State

For Sandy & Dave —
Happy food finds!
Hugs, Susan

BY SUSAN REIGLER
PHOTOGRAPHS BY PAM SPAULDING

Acclaim Press
MORLEY, MISSOURI

Acclaim Press
TM
— Your Next Great Book —

P.O. Box 238
Morley, MO 63767
(573) 472-9800
www.acclaimpress.com

Book and Cover Design: M. Frene Melton

Library of Congress Control Number: 2015903050
ISBN: 978-1-942613-00-8 / 1-942613-00-8

First Printing: 2015
Printed in the United States of America
10 9 8 7 6 5 4 3 2 1

This book was accuracy checked before printing, but the publisher is not responsible for errors or omissions. Recipes in this book were offered by the featured farms, restaurants, wineries, and businesses.

CONTENTS

$\mathcal{A}$CKNOWLEDGMENTS

$\mathcal{W}$e could not have written and photographed *Kentucky – Sweet & Savory* without the generous hospitality of all the farmers, chefs and restaurateurs, candy makers, distillers, brewers, bakers, cheese makers, wine producers, and other artisans featured in the book. Over and over we were impressed and gratified by their willingness to share their stories and the pride they take in their work. This is a heartfelt thanks for all of the time they spent with us.

Thanks also go to Genie Graf (Holly Hill Inn), Cindy Grisolia (Old Friends), Taylor Sang (Bourbon Barrel Foods) and Norma Taylor (Ruth Hunt Candies) for help they gave us in setting up tours and interviews. Thanks, too, to Kathy Cary (Lilly's Bistro) for permission to use her photo.

Finally, we very much appreciated the help our colleague from our days at the Louisville *Courier-Journal*, Sarah Fritschner, gave us in finding many of the people featured here. She is currently coordinator of Metro Louisville's Farm to Table Project, a splendid undertaking that seeks to expand the role of local producers in our hometown's food economy, https://louisvilleky.gov/government/louisville-forward/louisville-farm-table.

INTRODUCTION

The Bluegrass State's rich culinary tradition dates from pioneer days when the long hunters stalked wild turkey, deer, and bison. Throughout the 19th century, the foods of English, Scots, Irish and German settlers were modified into recipes using ingredients that could be grown on Kentucky farms. Foods and beverages that would become identified with Kentucky, including salt cured country ham, burgoo stew, red-eye gravy, and bourbon whiskey, evolved.

The goal of *Kentucky – Sweet & Savory* is to guide food lovers through this history by identifying places to enjoy traditional Kentucky dishes today. Included here are farm-to-table restaurants where chefs revel in using products that thrive in the state's mineral-rich limestone soil. These include everything from produce, such as heirloom tomatoes and sweet corn, to grass-fed beef, lamb, poultry, and pork.

Many producers of these goods are profiled, as well. In general, visitors are welcome at the farms and can purchase foodstuffs on site. Some other producers profiled sell at farmers' markets in Louisville, Lexington, and other cities. So there are many examples of where to buy authentic Kentucky products, too.

What was striking in visiting the farms and businesses, while reporting this book, was the remarkable number of third-, fourth-, and even fifth-generation farmers, innkeepers, millers, and craft distillers who proudly continue their family traditions today.

Speaking of distilleries, this is not a guide to visiting Kentucky's famous bourbon makers. But a few of the small, craft producers are profiled. Limits of space dictated that only a few examples of the nearly two dozen working distilleries in the state could be used. The situation is the same for wineries, of which there are now 70, and craft brewers who number about 30. The farm-to-table restaurant movement continues to grow, so it was impossible to include all of those establishments as well. Some hard choices had to be made.

You'll also find recipes throughout the book that show ways of using the bounty produced in Kentucky, from craft cocktails to main dishes and desserts. Whether visiting the locations described here, or trying your hand at a recipe, I hope you will enjoy savoring the flavors of Kentucky.

REGIONAL MAP

Featured within these pages are a variety of establishments.

Each region represented sends the adventurer on a journey through several Kentucky cities, spanning several counties.

Bluegrass Region

Anderson County • *Lawrenceburg*
Bourbon County • *Paris*
Boyle County • *Danville*
Clark County • *Winchester*
Fayette County • *Lexington*
Franklin County • *Frankfort*
Garrard County • *Lancaster*
Lincoln County • *Stanford*
Mercer County • *Harrodsburg, Salvisa*
Scott County • *Georgetown*
Woodford County • *Midway, Versailles*

Louisville Region

Jefferson County • *Louisville*
LaRue County • *Hodgenville*
Marion County • *Gravel Switch, Lebanon*
Meade County • *Payneville*
Shelby County • *Finchville, Shelbyville, Simpsonville*

Northern River Region

Bracken County • *Augusta*
Campbell County • *California, Camp Springs*
Kenton County • *Erlanger, Morning View*
Mason County • *Maysville*
Owen County • *Owenton*
Trimble County • *Bedford*

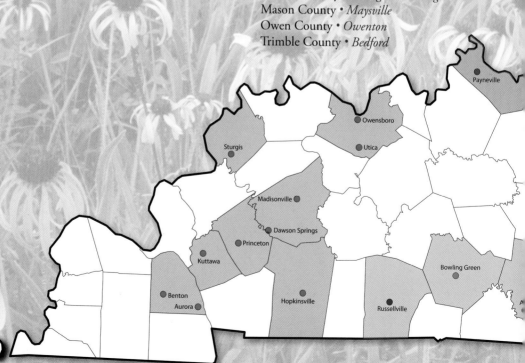

Eastern Region

Bath County • *Salt Lick*
Estill County • *Irvine*
Greenup County • *South Shore*
Harlan County • *Cumberland*
Laurel County • *London*
Letcher County • *Oven Fork*
Madison County • *Berea*
McCreary County • *Whitley City*
Montgomery County • *Jeffersonville,
    Mt. Sterling*
Morgan County • *West Liberty*
Rockcastle County • *Climax*
Wolfe County • *Campton*

South Central Region

Barren County • *Austin*
Logan County • *Russellville*
Monroe County • *Fountain Run*
Warren County • *Bowling Green*

Western Region

Caldwell County • *Dawson Springs,
    Princeton*
Christian County • *Hopkinsville*
Daviess County • *Owensboro, Utica*
Hopkins County • *Madisonville*
Lyon County • *Kuttawa*
Marshall County • *Aurora, Benton*
Union County • *Sturgis*

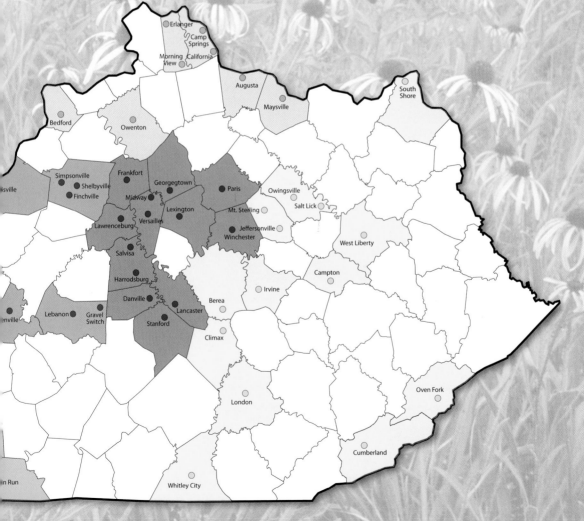

BLUEGRASS REGION

Frankfort
Midway
Georgetown
Lexington
Paris
Lawrenceburg
Versailles
Salvisa
Winchester
Harrodsburg
Danville
Lancaster
Stanford

Rebecca Ruth Candy
116 E. Second Street
Frankfort, KY 40601
(502) 223-7475
www.rebeccaruth.com

Monday - Saturday:
  10 a.m. - 6 p.m.
Sunday:
  12 p.m. - 6 p.m.

may randomly shadow a tour group. It's part of his quality control routine, which includes checking on the heat of the fire under a copper pot of liquid candy or seeing that the supply of pecans to top the bourbon ball candies is adequate.

Much of the equipment used in making Booe's candy is decades old, including the marble slabs for cooling brittle and copper kettles, which provide even heat for melting ingredients. Even older equipment is on display in a small candy museum situated between the shop and the factory. A 14-foot long stone and marble table dating from 1854 was used by Ruth Booe and survived not one, but two fires.

Ruth Booe came up with the bourbon ball in 1938 and today's candies are made with her original recipe. Charles Booe reveals, when asked, that the bourbon used in Rebecca Ruth chocolates is Evan Williams 100 proof. (Any lower proof bourbon might be hidden by the sugar and chocolate. It's a tricky balance.)

Rebecca Ruth's fame may be based on bourbon balls, but the oldest type of candy sold here is the Mint Kentucky Colonel, the confection on which the company was founded. These are minty dark chocolates containing a roasted pecan.

The 30-minute tour ends with a complementary bourbon ball. But the shop is filled with a wide variety of delicious, handmade chocolates, caramels, and other sweets. Happily, for the indecisive, sampler boxes are available.

BAUER'S CANDIES
Makers of the Modjeska
LAWRENCEBURG

*H*elena Modjeska (1840-1909) was a Polish-born actress who toured Europe and America specializing in Shakespeare's tragedies and other serious dramas. Among the actors with whom she played were Edwin Booth, Maurice Barrymore, and Joseph Haworth. Madame Helena, as she was known by her admirers, arrived in Louisville in 1883 where she starred in the American premier of Ibsen's *A Doll's House*. One of the playgoers enthralled by her performance was Anton Busath, a local candy maker so taken with Madame Helena that he was inspired to invent a decadent confection that, with her permission, he named in her honor.

When Busath Candies closed in 1947, Bauer's Candies became the premier makers of the Modjeska, a marshmallow-filled caramel treat that current company head, fourth generation candy maker Anna Bauer Satterwhite says are "made with the richest ingredients."

Tasting is believing.

Each hand-made Modjeska comes individually wrapped in wax paper. The buttery caramel surrounding the springy marshmallow center is thick and chewy. Two or three bites that comprise each candy are almost as filling as a meal.

Bauer's was headquartered in Louisville until it moved several years ago to its current factory location in a small industrial park outside of Lawrenceburg. Visitors are welcome to tour the candy-making floor where caramel is melted in big copper bowls, then poured into dishes from which candy makers spoon it over each marshmallow center. The caramel is then

ANNA – EASTER AD
5 YEARS OLD

painted evenly to form the biscuit-shaped pieces. After the caramel cools, each candy is wrapped to maintain freshness.

In addition to the original Modjeska, there is a chocolate version. Bauer's also makes vanilla and chocolate caramels – every one luscious.

According to Satterwhite, most of the company's business is online through mail order, though it's not too hard to find the candies at gourmet specialty stores in Louisville and Lexington. She says she has shipped Modjeskas all over the world, to as far away

Bauer's Candies
1103 Dylan Drive
Lawrenceburg, KY 40342
(502) 839-3700 or (877) 622-8377
www.bauerscandy.com
Fourth generation candy maker.

June - August
  Monday - Thursday:
  8 a.m. - 3 p.m.

September - May
  Monday - Friday:
  8 a.m. - 4:30 p.m.

as Europe and China. She even has a standing annual order from a titled family in England. (It would not be hard to imagine the aristocrats in *Downton Abbey* indulging in these elegant sweets with their afternoon tea.)

Devotees of the eponymous candy also refer to them as "Majestics," since Modjeska may be a bit of a tongue tier. But honestly, it shouldn't be that difficult to pronounce. Especially considering that the actress's full name was actually "Modrzejewska."

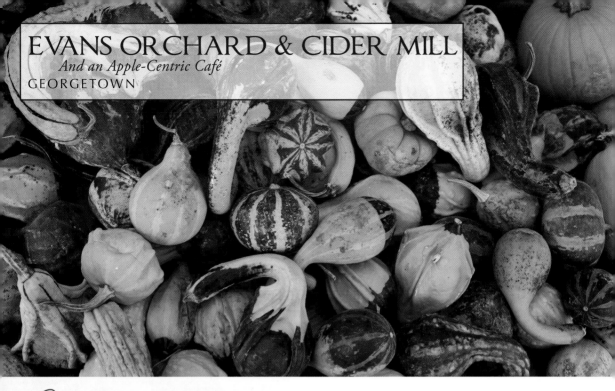

EVANS ORCHARD & CIDER MILL
And an Apple-Centric Café
GEORGETOWN

As has been the case with many Kentucky farming families, Kevan and Sue Evans and their daughter Jenny have turned to new crops for their land. Kevan Evans' great-great-grandfather first farmed here, raising cattle and what was then Kentucky's most important export, burley tobacco.

When the negative health effects of smoking were finally acknowledged and tobacco production was greatly scaled back in the 1990s, the family repurposed their 175 acres by planting 15 with apple, pear, and peach trees, 20 in vegetables, and a couple in strawberries and blueberries. They converted the to-bacco barn to a visitors' center and farm market. And they built a playground and picnic area welcoming families with children, who are clearly always fascinated to watch apple cider being made.

The cider mill is central to the Evans Orchard operation. Apples are squeezed, filtered and turned into cider not just from here but, because Evans has a pasteurizing facility, cider is also produced from their apples for several orchards around the region. Visitors can watch the process, which starts with the pulping of bushels of apples and the release of their fruity fragrance into the air of the facility. Sweet, fresh cider samples cap the show. But as important as cider is to the operation, that's only one form in which visitors can enjoy the fruit.

Evans' apples are used in apple cider doughnuts (and doughnut holes), apple dumplings, fried apple pies, caramel apples, baked apple pies, and even to flavor pulled pork barbecue sandwiches served in the orchard's Sweet Apple Café and Bakery. The café is housed in the shed next the farm market. Besides the apple-inflected items, the menu includes hot dogs, hamburgers, grilled chicken, rib-eye sandwiches, and homemade fudge in several flavors.

A trip to the orchard is also an opportunity to shop for more than two dozen kinds of vegetables grown on the farm, a variety of preserves made from orchard fruit, honey made by bees that pollinate the fruit trees and, of course, all the baked goods. By the way, the apple cider cake doughnuts are outstandingly moist and sprinkled with cinnamon. They may be every bit as addictive as tobacco, but obviously better for

Evans Orchard & Cider Mill
180 Stone Road
Georgetown, KY 40324
(502) 863-2255
www.evansorchard.com

May - November
  Tuesday - Saturday:
    9:30 a.m. - 6 p.m.
  Sunday:
    12 p.m. - 6 p.m.

you. Cindy Peake, of Bramble Ridge Orchard, developed the recipe. (See p. 120)

For the complete farm experience, visit in the fall for U-Pick apples (there are more than 20 varieties) and to choose a pumpkin from the popular pumpkin patch. If, for some reason, you can't visit the orchard, you can find Evans' fruit and produce (and those doughnuts) at the Lexington Farmers Market.

*I*t is impossible to travel around central Kentucky and not drive past acre after acre of the region's iconic horse farms. Even a drive along Interstate 64 affords views of emerald-green, fence-enclosed pastures populated by grazing and frolicking Thoroughbreds.

Horses can live to be 25 or 30 years old. But the reality of racing is that most are retired much earlier. Equine athletes, just like their human counterparts, risk injury the longer they compete. So the winners of the Grade I stakes races, such as the Kentucky Derby and Breeders Cup contests, often retire from racing at an early age to take up residence on breeding farms. They can make more money for their owners by producing new generations than by racing.

But what happens to these champions after they finish their careers as parents? Sadly, a lot of Thoroughbreds, even famous ones, meet undistinguished ends.

Horse lovers were stunned and saddened in 2002 when it was reported that Ferdinand, the 1986 Kentucky Derby winner and 1987 Horse of the Year, had died in a Japanese slaughterhouse. The 19-year-old horse became dog food, after his career, on a Japanese stud farm was deemed over.

Former *Boston Globe* movie critic and racing fan Michael Blowen was one of the people deeply moved by Ferdinand's fate. Shortly after the horse's death was reported, he started Old Friends, a retirement farm for Thoroughbreds. More than a decade later, the Kentucky facility is home to over 100 horses, including Popcorn Deelites, one of eight horses who played Seabiscuit in the 2003 film, and Silver Charm, winner of the Kentucky Derby and the Preakness Stakes in 1997.

Blowen himself leads most of the tours around the farm, introducing the horses to delighted visitors. He explains that the reason so many horses were needed to play Seabiscuit is that "The horse who played War Admiral [who Seabiscuit upset in a famous match race], kept winning during the filming. So they had to keep bringing in fresh Seabiscuits!"

His love of his charges is infectious. When the equine residents crane their heads over fences and nuzzle visitors, adults and children, both delight in following Blowen's example, feeding horses treats from a bucket he carries on the tour. But no one else indulges in Blowen's trick of putting a carrot in his mouth to be lifted gently from his lips by Catlaunch, a gelding who earned over $1 million during his racing career.

Old Friends Farm
1841 Paynes Depot Road
Georgetown, KY 40324
(502) 863-1775
www.oldfriendsequine.prg

Tours April - October
(Reservations Required)
    Daily: 10 a.m., 1 p.m., 3 p.m.

Tours November - March
(Reservations Required)
    Daily: 11 a.m. only

The 137-acre farm also has a thriving population of barn cats, a few goat companions for some of the Thoroughbreds, and another horse named Silver Charm who, thanks to his size, will not be confused with the Derby winner.

Little Silver Charm is a miniature horse with a bright, white mane who bestows horsey kisses on Blowen as visitors look on. He looks as though he would be right at home in Middle Earth, being just about the right sized mount for a hobbit.

Old Friends is a not-for-profit operation and so relies on tour fees, gift shop sales, and donations to maintain its retirees. The service the farm has brought to its residents was acknowledged in 2014 when Old Friends was presented with a Special Eclipse Award from the National Thoroughbred Racing Association, the American horse racing industry's highest honor.

BOUR-BON
Farm-to-Table Dining and Live Music
PARIS

$\mathcal{P}$aris, named in honor of the French capital, is the county seat of Bourbon County, named in honor of the French royal family. Bluegrass Francophilia, resulting from the aid given by the French to America during the Revolutionary War, is also reflected in the names of Louisville (honoring King Louis XVI) and Versailles (pronounced "ver-sales" by locals).

Main Street of Paris, Kentucky, will not be mistaken for one of the boulevards of Paris, France. But it has both 19th century architectural charm and a café society, courtesy of a new restaurant.

Proprietor Joseph Clay, a descendant of Kentucky's famous statesman Henry Clay, chose to name his latest eatery Bour-Bon, both as a nod to his home county and the bounty of local foods produced on its farms. (*Bon* being the French word meaning "good.")

Thanks to alcohol sales finally being permitted in Bourbon County (which ironically, may have been the geographic origin – or not – of the famous corn-based whiskey), the restaurant also has an impressive craft cocktail program. Naturally, it features several bourbon–based drinks, both classics, such as the Manhattan, and original creations. One of these is the Dark Side, made with both bourbon and rye from Bulleit, Bonal (a French aperitif), mint, lime, bitters, and simple syrup. Topped up with soda and served over ice, it's both refreshing and potent.

General Manager Glenn DeLong can often be found behind the 36-foot long zinc bar that takes up one side of the atmospheric main dining room furnished with Louis XVI style chairs and tables and decorated in soft blues and greys. His custom mixing techniques include heating a lemon peel to release its oils before using it to garnish an Old Fashioned. (Yes, the cocktails here may take a little longer to make than in many bars. Patience is, however, greatly rewarded.)

The dinner menu is indeed "bon," stocked with good dishes slowly roasted in the restaurant's wood-fired oven built in Argentina. It is housed in a building next to the main restaurant on one side of a

Country Boy Brewing
436 Chair Avenue
Lexington, KY 40508
(859) 554-6200
www.countryboybrewing.com

Monday - Saturday:
12 a.m. - 12 a.m.
Sunday:
12 p.m. - 10 p.m.

Country Boy Brewing

Country Boy is a few minutes' walk from Rupp Arena, tucked away down a short street in an industrial area. The small taproom boasts 24 taps, mostly featuring the beers made in the adjoining brewery, but offering some guests, too. Partners Jeff Beagle (brewery manager), Evan Coppage (brewer), and Daniel Harrison (general manager) have a commitment to using locally grown hops (from Revolutionary Hop Farm in Carter County) and other Kentucky grown vegetables and fruits. To date, they've made more than 70 beers, including regular offerings Cliff Jumper IPA, Amos Moses Brown Ale, and Cougar Bait Blonde, and less mainstream brews Jalapeno Smoked Porter, Nacho Bait (fruit & vegetable beer), and Danger Cherry Stout.

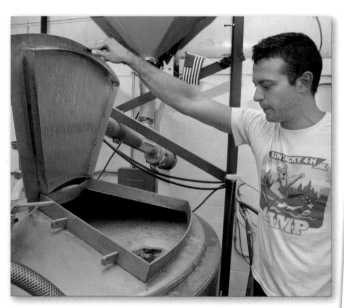

Blue Stallion Brewing Co.
610 W. Third Street
Lexington, KY 40508
(877) 928-2337
www.bluestallionbrewing.com

Monday - Thursday:
 4 p.m. - 11 p.m.
Friday - Saturday:
 12 p.m. - 10 p.m.
Sunday:
 12 p.m. - 10 p.m.

Blue Stallion Brewing Co.

One of **Blue Stallion's** five partners is German-born head brewer Nico Schulz. So not surprisingly a variety of German lagers are brewed here, including Dunkel, Pilsner, Hefeweizen, and Schwarzbier. Among seasonal selections are Maibock, Doppelbock, and Oktoberfest. Schulz also enjoys making British ales, so look for a variety of traditional bitters and Scottish ales such as Wee Heavy and Scottish 70 Shilling. The large, modern brew house can be seen through the wall of the main room where the taps are found, behind a tall bar made from bourbon barrel staves. The other Stallion partners are brothers Kore, Zac, and Xavier Donnelly, and Jim Clemons.

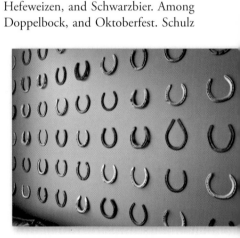

West Sixth Brewing &
Smithtown Seafood
501 W. Sixth Street
Lexington, KY 40508
(859) 705-0915
www.westsixth.com

Monday - Wednesday:
  11 a.m. - 10 p.m.
Thursday:
  11 a.m. - 11 p.m.
Friday - Saturday:
  11 a.m. - 12 a.m.
Sunday:
  11 a.m. - 10 p.m.

Tours
  Saturday: 2 p.m., 4 p.m.
  Sunday: 2 p.m.

West Sixth Brewing & Smithtown Seafood

Several businesses share the multi-story space where **West Sixth Brewing** occupies most of the ground floor. Conveniently, one of Ouita Michel's eateries, **Smithtown Seafood**, is also on the ground floor and accessible directly from the taproom. So a symbiosis exists between the brewery, with no kitchen of its own, and the seafood counter and market, which is take-out only.

Settle into a seat at the bar or at one of the handful of tables after ordering from Smithtown. You'll receive a number on a metal stand and someone from Smithtown will bring over your food. While waiting, get your beer. The sampler is highly recommended so you can try out five West Sixth's head brewer Robin Sither's standards – West Sixth IPA, Deliberation Amber, Lemongrass American Wheat, Pay It Forward Cocoa Porter, and Smithtown Brown. The can't-miss selection from the Smithtown menu is the addictively crispy fish and chips (with hushpuppies and slaw), served in a large enough portion to share, especially if you are leaving room for more beer.

Beer lovers interested in the nuts and bolts of the operation will want to take a brewery tour, offered Saturdays at 2 and 4 p.m. and Sundays at 2 p.m.

25

LEXINGTON FARMERS MARKET
Established in 1975
LEXINGTON

Situated in the heart of downtown, the Lexington Farmers Market's Saturday home is a Victorian glass and steel pavilion reminiscent of London's Covent Garden, but usually warmer and sunnier. Farmers and vendors from throughout the Bluegrass region – and sometimes beyond – crowd into the plaza offering cut flowers, seasonal fruits and vegetables, fresh eggs, artisan cheeses, freshly-squeezed juices, locally roasted coffee, local wines, vinegars and olive oils, local honey, artisan ice cream, fresh baked goods, herbs (fresh and potted), pasture-fed meat, and even hand-made dog treats, which explains why there are as many dogs on leashes as children in strollers on any given Saturday.

Two of the producers especially worth seeking out, since their unique farms are not open for public tours, are Elmwood Stock Farm of Georgetown (www.elmwoodstockfarm.com) and The Paw Paw Plantation, located in Stanton near Red River Gorge.

Sixth generation farmers Ann and Mac Stone are two of the proprietors of Elmwood, which has long provided premium Black Angus cattle breeding stock to beef producers in Kentucky. Ann's brother John, his wife Melissa, and John's father Cecil Bell and his wife Kay, also tend the 375-acre farm, which is home to other organically certified, pasture-raised livestock, too. In addition to the Angus, the meat produced and available at the Farmers' Market comes from Dorset-Suffolk-crossed sheep; Bronze, Narragansett, Royal Palm, and Grey Slate turkeys, and Red Star and Cornish Cross chickens. Additionally, the Stones cultivate a wide array of fruits and vegetables and offer CSA subscriptions.

Lexington Farmers Market
Cheapside Park, Cheapside Street
(between Main and Short Streets)
Lexington, KY 40507
(859) 608-2655
www.lexingtonfarmersmarket.com

Saturday (Spring/Summer/Fall):
7 a.m. - 2 p.m.
Saturday (Winter):
8 a.m. - 1 p.m.
See our website for other days and locations.

Look for the Stones behind their multicolored display of baby spinach, chard, peppers – green, red, yellow and orange –, okra, heirloom tomatoes, and corn. Coolers behind the table laden with produce and eggs hold their various meats.

From his name, it would be fitting if Roland McIntosh grew apples. But his fruit is the pawpaw, sweet, oblong, pulpy fruit with a flavor that's a little hard to pin down. Some liken it to a cross between a banana and a very sweet pear. McIntosh says it's "a pineapple-mango mix." He also calls it "a power fruit" since it's "chock full of nutrients and anti-oxidants, like blueberries."

The fruit grows on slender trees native to the eastern United States, though most of its relatives are tropical. It's hypothetically possible to eat pawpaws picked straight from a tree growing in the woods, but good luck getting a ripe one before the raccoons, opossums, squirrels, foxes, and other animals that relish the fruit get them first.

McIntosh has been growing pawpaws for three decades and his farm currently has about 1,100 trees from which he harvests some 800 pounds of fruit annually. He brings them to the Lexington Farmers Market from late August to mid-October and also sells seedling trees, offering advice on cultivation.

When asked by a pawpaw neophyte how good the fruit really is, Roland McIntosh has a pretty good answer, "I've been selling them to a lot of fancy restaurants for more than 20 years."

Pawpaw Bread

This comes from a set of pawpaw recipes printed on Kentucky State University's website, www.pawpaw.kysu.edu/pawpaw/recipes.htm. It originated in Mark F. Sohn's Mountain Country Cooking, St. Martin's Press, New York, 1996.

1 c. melted butter
2 c. sugar
4 eggs
2 c. pawpaw pulp
1 T. lemon juice
4 c. sifted all-purpose flour
2 t. baking powder
3 c. pecan pieces plus 16 pecan halves

• Preheat oven to 375 degrees F. Grease two 9x4x2-inch loaf pans.
• Beat together butter, sugar, and eggs. Add and beat in the pawpaw pulp and lemon juice.
• Sift the flour and baking powder together, and stir them into the batter. Stir in the pecans and scrape the batter into the loaf pans.
• Garnish each loaf with 8 pecan halves, and bake for 1 hour and 15 minutes. The top corners of the loaf will burn, but that adds flavor and character.

WINDY CORNER MARKET
Farm-to-Table Café Surrounded by Horse Farms
LEXINGTON

Windy Corner has a deceptively rural location. Both the tall windows of the main dining room and the tables nestled onto a cozy screened porch afford tranquil views of Bluegrass horse farms. But Ouita Michel's food market and casual café is a short 20 minutes from downtown Lexington.

From almost any approach, the drive to the restaurant meanders along roads lined with dry stone or plank fences, and past manicured horse farms and glimpses of historic mansions, churches, and barns. This is the genteel landscape that the Bluegrass Conservancy, www.bluegrassconservancy.org, and other concerned Kentuckians are striving to save from suburban sprawl.

The clapboard-sided building perched at the corner of Muir Station and Bryan Station Roads sports a cheerfully painted mural and, in summer, features flowerbeds teeming with colorful native flora. While the setting is quiet, the restaurant itself is bustling almost all the time, from early morning breakfast to late evening dinner.

A perfect Kentucky start to the day would be breakfast of thinly sliced Browning's Country Ham (from Dry Ridge) and red-eye gravy served with eggs, red-skin hash brown potatoes, Weisenberger stone ground grits (from Midway), and a buttermilk biscuit. Bacon and sausage come from Stone Cross Farms (near Taylorsville) and the Belgian waffles are served with Country Rock Maple Syrup (Versailles).

Kentucky ingredients are also used as often as possible on the lunch and dinner menu which includes pulled pork and roast beef sandwiches; seafood baskets (piled high with fried oysters, shrimp, catfish or crawfish) served with hush puppies and fries and slaw; and seared salmon and rib-eye steak entrees. The beverage selection includes bottled Kentucky Ale.

Windy Corner Market
4595 Bryan Station Road
Lexington, KY 40516
(859) 294-9338
www.windycornermarket.com

Monday - Friday:
 7 a.m. - 8:30 p.m.
Saturday - Sunday:
 9 a.m. - 8:30 p.m.

Families will be pleased to know there's a "Kid's Choice Menu." Selections include a white cheddar whole grain quesadilla, a trio of corncakes topped with pulled pork, and a mini beef burger served on a whole-wheat bun. No chips here. Instead, there's a choice of steamed veggies of the day, a small salad, or carrot and celery sticks.

Customers order at a counter from Windy Corner's very efficient staff. The large, light main room of the market/restaurant is made even more cheerful by rows of colorful jockeys' silks hanging near the ceiling on the yellow bead board walls. During peak times, it can be a bit of a challenge to find a seat, but table turnover is fairly rapid, especially at lunch.

Many of the Kentucky-sourced ingredients used in the food served here, including cornmeal, syrups and preserves, can be found on the shelves lining the walls between the windows. Other items on the store shelves include regional cookbooks, greeting cards, equine art, and hand-painted glassware.

EQUUS RUN WINERY
Grapes Growing Next Door to Grazing Thoroughbreds
MIDWAY

*A*ppropriately for a Kentucky winery (and hence its name), Equus Run's 35 acres are located right next to a horse farm. It is literally possible to stand in the vineyard and see some of the Thoroughbreds at Margaux Farm grazing in the next pasture.

When Equus Run opened in 1998, it was one of only five or so licensed wineries in the state, so it has had time to build a reputation with wine drinkers. It also has a very accessible location, just a few minutes' drive from not one, but two interstate highway exits. Those are at least two of the reasons that Equus Run had some 44,000 visitors last year, making it one of the most visited Kentucky wineries. There are also Sunday evening concerts in a pur- pose-built amphitheater, special din- ners, and the fact that Equus Run is open all but three days of the year.

It also certainly doesn't hurt that the wine is very good.

The bestseller "by far," according to owner and winemaker Cynthia Bohn, is a rosé – Cabernet Sauvi- gnon Blanc de Noir. Given the pop- ularity of rosé, this may not seem surprising, except that most rosés usually are not made with cabernet sauvignon.

"It's my famous mistake wine," says Bohn with a laugh. "It was literally made by mistake – a little blending issue."

Bohn says that her next best sellers are the Ries- ling and the Merlot. These and at least a dozen wines, including Chardonnay, Cabernet Franc, and a des- sert wine dubbed Passionate Kiss (dark chocolate infused Cabernet Sauvignon with a hint of vanilla), can be found in the tasting room and shop, housed in a converted farm tool shed. Wines can be sampled and visitors can enjoy relaxing on the flower-bordered

Equus Run Winery
1280 Moores Mill Road
Midway, KY 40347
(859) 846-9463
www.equusrunvineyards.com

Monday - Friday:
  11 a.m. - 5 p.m.
    Fridays until 7 p.m. in summer
Saturday:
  11 a.m. - 7 p.m.
Sunday:
  1 p.m. - 5 p.m.

patio with a view of the vineyard. If you are looking for an outing, pack a lunch, buy a bottle of wine, and enjoy the garden picnic area. There's even a putting green if you are overcome with the urge to put in a little practice.

While grapes from the vineyard are used to make the wines here, Bohn also has to source fruit "from all over." Demand for Equus Run wines outgrew the capacity of the vineyards. So juice from other vineyards in Kentucky, as well as Indiana, Ohio, and Arkansas, and from as far away as New York, Oregon, and California, is fermented at the winery.

Bohn said that she's not alone in needing more grapes than she can grow. "A lot of growers are trying to keep up with the demand. The University of Kentucky agriculture researchers are investigating suitable grapes for our climate. Grapes are the high maintenance kids of fruits!"

Meanwhile, with close to two decades of experience, Bohn is still passionate about experimenting with new blends. "One of our visitors referred to me as 'the old grape lady'. Millennials!" While obviously amused rather than insulted, Bohn added, "I think I would prefer the word 'tenured'."

WALLACE STATION DELI & BAKERY
Horse Country Farm-to-Table
VERSAILLES

*N*estled along one of Kentucky's most scenic horse country roads, Wallace Station is definitely the place to get a feeling for day-to-day routine on the farms. Come here for lunch on a weekday and the popular restaurant is packed with exercise riders, grooms, and other horse farm personnel dressed in coveralls sporting their farms' logos. In other words, this is where the locals eat.

Listed on the National Register of Historic Places, the building dates from the turn of the 19th into the 20th century and contained a grocery and country store for decades. Ouita and Chris Michel opened it, their second venture after Holly Hill Inn, in 2003.

The interior is decorated with historic scenes of the horse farms, posters from equine competitions, and glass cases containing caps from neighboring farms. Tables with backed wooden benches are crammed closely together. Happily, the seating nearly doubles in good weather when tables on the back deck and the lawn are available.

The line for ordering forms alongside a case displaying fresh baked goods, which include sorghum cookies, lemon bars, scones, muffins, and cheesecake brownies. Order one of these to go to snack on while driving around the Bluegrass. Speaking of which, a real bonus here is the page on the back of the broadsheet menu describing how to visit the nearby horse farms. (Rule Number One – Call ahead.)

Breakfast is served all day. The menu includes classics such as a country ham or sausage biscuit, plus breakfast paninis and quiche. Lunch consists of a long list of generously portioned sandwiches, wraps, and burgers. Often two people can share one order. (Un-

Wallace Station Deli & Bakery
3854 Old Frankfort Pike
Versailles, KY 40383
(859) 846-5161
www.wallacestation.com

April - October
  Monday - Saturday:
    8 a.m. - 8 p.m.
  Sunday:
    8 a.m. - 6 p.m.

November - March
  Monday:
    8 a.m. - 8 p.m.
  Tuesday - Thursday:
    8 a.m. - 6 p.m.
  Saturday:
    7 a.m. - ?
  Sunday:
    8 a.m. - 6 p.m.

less, of course, you happened to have been putting racehorses through their exercise paces all morning.)

Among the most popular sandwiches are the Bourbon Trail Triple Crown (three stacked layers of turkey, cheddar, bacon, lettuce, and tomato), a six-ounce griddle-seared fish sandwich seasoned with smoked paprika, and chicken salad mixed with dried cranberries and almonds.

Wallace Station is a dinner destination on Monday and Friday nights when fried chicken and seafood are featured respectively. Choose portions from a half chicken to individual pieces, all served with two sides and a biscuit. Seafood is either Weisenberger beer-battered catfish, or fried oysters rolled in Weisenberger white cornmeal. Both dinners are served with fries, slaw, and hushpuppies.

The postal address is Versailles, but Wallace Station is located just a few minutes' drive south from downtown Midway. The town is popular with tourists for the shops lining the Main Street, which is bisected by the railroad track that runs down the middle of it.

33

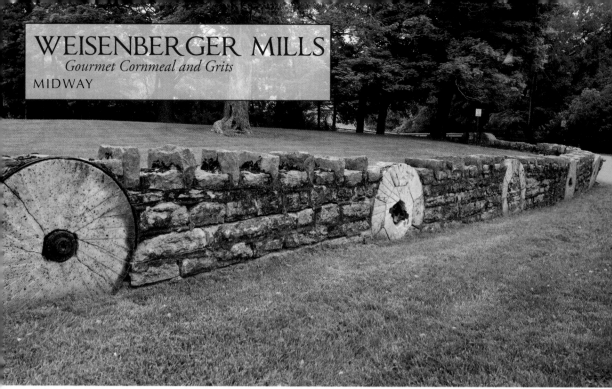

WEISENBERGER MILLS
Gourmet Cornmeal and Grits
MIDWAY

One of the reasons that the pioneer settlers found Kentucky such as good place to live was its abundance of water. The state has more miles of streams and rivers than any other but Alaska, which is, of course, many times larger in area. Historically, this running water provided not only transportation, but was an early source of power for the many mills that sprang up alongside the waterways.

Weisenberger Mills, on the outskirts of Midway, occupies a site on South Elkhorn Creek that has been home to a working mill for more than two centuries. German immigrant August Weisenberger bought the property in 1865 and his descendants still own and operate it today.

Weisenberger is the gold standard for cornmeal, grits, and flour in Kentucky, and its products, especially the grits, are identified by name on menus in the state's finest restaurants and beyond.

Travelers will know they are approaching the mill by the appearance of a low stone fence on the side of the road into which historic millstones have been imbedded. As the road curves to the left, the red brick mill building looms ahead, rising three stories above the creek. It is the oldest water-powered commercial flourmill in the state. Overseeing this grainy heritage is Philip Weisenberger, the sixth generation miller in his family.

He explains to visitors that the "modern" equipment, dating from 1913, is the machinery that supports the metal roller mill. This elaborate system of wheels and belts is responsible for grinding most of the grain here. It replaced the series of rods and

cogwheels that turned the heavy millstones in the 19th century. A small amount of stone grinding still happens here (of the products labeled "stone-ground"). The water wheel is gone. But thanks to the mill's electric turbines, water still generates the power for the machinery. The sound of the creek rushing over the spillway is almost as loud as the clamor of the metal inside the mill.

Most of the grain milled here is Kentucky-sourced. "The white corn comes from Hardin County," said Weisenberger. "And the yellow corn is from Shelby County."

Weisenberger Mills
2545 Weisenberger Mill Road
Midway, KY 40347
(859) 254-5282
www.weisenberger.com

Monday - Friday:
 8 a.m. - 4:30 p.m.
Saturday:
 9 a.m. - 12 p.m.

Visitors can buy all of Weisenberger Mills' products from a small shop in the front of the office. For home use, most of the flours and meals are in two or five pound bags. These include biscuit mix, various muffin mixes (apple cinnamon, lemon poppy seed, raspberry, yellow corn), hushpuppy mix, pancake mix, cornmeal, wheat flour, and, of course, the famous stone ground grits, both white and yellow varieties.

The loading dock next to the small parking lot has stacks of 25 pound commercial bags, destined for restaurants and bakers not only in Kentucky, but well beyond. "We have customers in New York, Chicago, Denver, all over," remarks Weisenberger. And the farthest his grits have traveled? "We've shipped to Hawaii and Saudi Arabia."

Basic Cheese Grits Casserole

Cheese grits are de rigueur *at Kentucky Derby brunches and, indeed, at just about any brunch across the Bluegrass State. This is the Weisenberger recipe.*

4 c. water
1 c. grits
½ t. salt
2 T. butter
1 c. shredded cheese
2 slightly beaten eggs (in a separate bowl)

- Add ½ teaspoon salt to 4 cups water and bring to a boil in a large saucepan. Add 1 cup grits, stir, reduce heat to a simmer, cover, and cook for 20 minutes, stirring often.
- When grits are done, add the butter to the grits and stir or whisk until melted. Then add about ½ cup of hot grits to the beaten eggs and mix thoroughly; then immediately add the egg mixture to the pot of hot grits and stir/whisk together.
- Add the cheese and stir until melted.
- Pour this mixture into a greased 8x8-inch baking dish and cook in a preheated 350 degrees F. oven for 1 hour or until lightly browned on top. Refrigerate any leftovers.

This is a basic recipe. Other options might be to add 1 clove of chopped garlic, use ½ milk and ½ water, or ½ chicken broth and ½ water. You can use any cheese that melts well.

This recipe can be doubled and baked in a greased 9x13-inch baking dish.

35

ALE-8-ONE
Kentucky's Indigenous Soft Drink
WINCHESTER

*I*n addition to beer cheese, Winchester has another claim to Kentucky food history fame. It is home to an original state beverage. No, not bourbon. Soda pop maker G. L. Wainscott invented Ale-8-One, a gingery, carbonated soft drink, here in 1926.

Wainscott had started his carbonated beverage business more than 20 years before. In 1906, he introduced Roxa-Kola, which proved popular enough to make its famous competitor, Coca-Cola, nervous. Coke sued and Wainscott decided that it would be prudent to look for a different signature flavor.

As a short introductory film recounts at the beginning of a guided tour of the Ale-8 manufacturing and bottling plant, Wainscott searched for a new flavor idea on a trip to northern Europe. A popular soft drink there was ginger beer, a more robust cousin to ginger ale. Wainscott came home with a new formula and his ginger-flavored soda was launched.

But what should it be called?

Wainscott sponsored a naming contest that year at the Clark County Fair. The winning entry was "A Late One," to say that this was the latest thing in soft drinks. In what may count as the Kentucky version of Cockney rhyming slang, the drink was dubbed "Ale-8-One." It's been a local favorite ever since. Indeed, who wouldn't be drawn to a beverage that once had as its marketing tag line, "It Glorifies"?

Ale-8-One
25 Carol Road
Winchester, KY 40391
(859) 744-3484
www.ale8one.com

Monday - Friday:
  8:30 a.m. - 4:30 p.m.
  Call for tour information and reservations.

Also during the introduction to the plant tour, the guide passes around a stopped flask of the Ale-8-One syrup formula. It is potently spicy. The soda produced from it is sweeter and spicier than ginger ale, but not quite as bodacious as ginger beer.

The free tour includes a short walk into the plant where visitors can see the bottling line through a glass-walled room. It concludes with a stop by a refrigerator stocked with 12-ounce bottles of the drink and one is given to each person on the tour.

Before leaving, visitors are encouraged to spend some time in the gift shop, which is stocked not only with bottled soft drinks (a diet version is now available, too), but also with apparel (tee-shirts, hoodies, caps) sporting the green, red, and white Ale-8-One logo, as do bar trays, key chains, glassware and more.

Ale-8-One is also no longer just a Kentucky drink. Today, G. L. Wainscott's great-great nephew, Fielding Rogers, runs the family-owned company and the soda is distributed throughout much of Ohio and Indiana, as well as most of Kentucky. And the company Ale-8-One contracts with and relies upon for this distribution? Ironically, none other than Coca-Cola.

Hot Wings with Ale-8-One Dipping Sauce

This recipe was the entree winner in the 2006 recipe competition among Sullivan University culinary students.

Wings
1 lb. chicken wings
1 12-oz. bottle Ale-8-One
2 T. hot sauce
2 T. pineapple juice
1 yellow onion, medium dice
Pinch of ground ginger
1 T. garlic salt
¼ c. canola or peanut oil for frying

Dipping Sauce
Reduce 1 12-oz. bottle Ale-8-One by half.
Stir in:
2 T. honey
2 T. molasses
2 T. hot sauce
1 T. soy sauce
1 t. tomato paste
Cayenne pepper to taste
Reduce by half or until sauce becomes syrupy.

• Combine all ingredients except chicken wings until thoroughly mixed.
• Add wings and marinate 1 hour.
• Remove excess marinade from wings and lightly toss in: 1 cup flour and 1 cup cornstarch, combined.
• Deep fry for 8-10 minutes at 350 degrees F.

BEAUMONT INN
Quintessential Kentucky Bed & Breakfast
HARRODSBURG

$\mathcal{H}$elen and Chuck Dedman and their son Dixon are the fourth and fifth generations of proprietors to welcome guests to the gracious Beaumont Inn, which became a hotel in 1917. The three-story red brick Greek Revival mansion, complete with six stately white columns, dates from 1845, and much of its ante-bellum heritage remains intact.

Just inside the front door, the entrance hall walls are lined with framed portraits of Civil War generals. The main parlor, to the left of the hall, is furnished with Victorian antiques, handmade Irish linen curtains, and a Steinway piano dating from the time 1856 to 1917 that the house operated as a girls' preparatory school. Beaumont College's motto: "Exalted character graced by elegant culture and refined manners."

Don't worry. While shorts are only permitted in the dining room at breakfast and lunch, guests do not actually have to "dress" for dinner. But the traditional Southern cuisine – fried chicken, corn pudding, aged country ham – served in the dining room overlooking the inn's tree-shaded gardens, harkens back to a more genteel lifestyle. The restaurant is open to the public, as well as to inn guests, who can stay in the main building itself with its antiques-furnished rooms, or in two other guesthouses on the Beaumont's grounds.

"Activities" might be a strong word to describe how to pass the time here. A stroll along the paths on the grounds is leisurely. There is a shuffleboard court, and a swimming pool, but most guests are more drawn to the rocking chairs on the front porch with a view of old hickory, walnut, and catalpa trees.

The Beaumont complex also contains a couple of more casual eateries, The Old Owl Tavern and the Owl's Nest Pub. Why owls?

Before Prohibition, and before they became innkeepers, members of the Dedman family operated the Kentucky Owl distillery. That history is honored in the bars' names and also by the recent release of a

Beaumont Inn
638 Beaumont Inn Drive
Harrodsburg, KY 40330
(859) 734-3381
www.beaumontinn.com

Main Dining Room
Wednesday - Friday:
  11:30 a.m. - 1:30 p.m.,
  6 p.m - 7:30 p.m.
Saturday:
  6 p.m. - 8 p.m.
Sunday:
  11: a.m. - 1:30 p.m.

Old Owl Tavern
Monday - Thursday:
  4 p.m. - 9 p.m.
Friday:
  4 p.m. - 10 p.m.
Saturday:
  11:30 am - 10 p.m.

Owl's Nest Pub
Wednesday - Saturday:
  5 p.m. - 10 p.m.

limited production, small batch of new Kentucky Owl bourbon. With the family's distilling history and the inn's close proximity to several of central Kentucky's modern distilleries, the Beaumont Inn is a great place to stay while exploring Bourbon Country.

After a day of touring, check out the list of more than 70 bourbons available at the two Owls. Flights (a sampler of several drinks) are available. But for a special experience, book a private tasting with Dixon Dedman. He often conducts these in the comfortable James Harrod Room in the main building. In the Profile Tasting, Dedman describes the characteristic flavors found in the bourbons of several distilleries. The tasting of ultra premium Bourbons features whiskies that are often hard to find. Know that you need to book one of these popular tastings well in advance of a visit. When asked about the success of his program, Dedman was gratified. "I had no idea how these would take off!"

Beaumont Inn's Famous Corn Pudding
This is the inn's most requested recipe.

2 c. white whole kernel corn, or fresh corn cut off the cob
4 eggs
8 level T. flour
1 qt. milk
4 rounded t. sugar
4 T. butter, melted
1 t. salt

- Stir into the corn the flour, salt, sugar, and butter.
- Beat the eggs well, put them into the milk, then stir into the corn mixture and put into a pan or Pyrex dish. Bake in oven at 450 degrees F. for about 40-45 minutes.
- Stir vigorously with a long pronged fork three times, approximately 10 minutes apart while baking, disturbing the top as little as possible.

SHAKER VILLAGE OF PLEASANT HILL
Making You "Kindly Welcome"
HARRODSBURG

When the legendary R. W. "Johnny" Apple, Jr. of the *New York Times* visited Kentucky in 1998 as his newspaper's food and travel correspondent, he spent time in Louisville museums, restaurants, and in central Kentucky's distilleries. And he concluded his article, published on October 23rd of that year, with this advice:

"If you have more time, spend a morning in the more abstemious atmosphere of the restored Shaker Village of Pleasant Hill, near Harrodsburg. The triumph of the place is not the 33 brick, frame and stone buildings, or the clever, handsome furniture, or even the wonderful twin spiral staircases at the Trustees' House. The triumph is the sense of serenity – or is it spirituality? – that visitors feel, far from the roar of the interstate and the clamor of the city, surrounded by ponds and meadows where sheep may safely graze."

It will actually take you much more than a morning to appreciate all that Shaker Village has to offer. The carefully restored buildings are situated on 3000 acres of prime central Bluegrass landscape bordered by the winding Kentucky River. It includes 40 miles of trails through a nature preserve (home to 125 species of nesting and migrating birds, including quail), a working farm among the buildings Apple mentioned, a tobacco barn now converted to serve as a concert hall when the Chamber Music Society of Lincoln Center visits every Memorial Day weekend, and a seed-to-table restaurant. Guests can stay overnight in most of the buildings, which offer first class accommodations.

In 1805, Elisha Thomas and Henry and Samuel Banta of Mercer County attended a revival meeting in which they were converted to the United Society for Believers in Christ's Second Appearance (more commonly known as "Shakers" for their exuberant worship services). The following year they and more than 40 other converts founded a settlement on Thomas' farm and began to build the community that became known as Pleasant Hill.

The Shakers were excellent craftsmen who fashioned elegantly simple and very functional furniture. The symmetrical buildings all have separate

Shaker Village of Pleasant Hill
3501 Lexington Road
Harrodsburg, KY 40330
(859) 734-5411
www.shakervillageky.org

Trustees' Dining Room
Daily:
7:30 a.m. - 10 a.m.,
11:30 a.m - 3 p.m.,
5 p.m. - 8:30 p.m.

entrances for men and women because the sect practiced celibacy, which turned out to be about the only aspect of their community that lacked practicality. By 1910, the population of the settlement had diminished from about 500 at its height, to 12.

Even if you can't enjoy an extended stay, do try to eat here. Much of the produce served in the restaurant is grown in the village's farm gardens. Salsify, a root vegetable brought to America by European settlers, is used in a signature casserole. Also called "oyster plant," the casserole tastes not unlike a vegetarian version of oyster stuffing.

"The lemon pie is the truest Shaker recipe we have here," says David Larson, a retired chef and Shaker Village's Vice President of Retail Operations. "They traded goods along the rivers all the way to New Orleans so they could get lemons. The recipe reflects their philosophy of leaving nothing behind. Every part of the lemon is used."

The tangy pie is a lemon-lover's delight. It has the texture of a chess pie, but with serious citrus attitude.

Alcohol sales have become legal in Mercer County since Apple's visit, so visitors no longer have to be "abstemious" and can enjoy beer or wine, or even bourbon, with a meal. But the historic village and farm, grazing sheep and all, remains blissfully tranquil.

Shaker Lemon Pie

This signature dessert of Shaker Village at Pleasant Hill probably originated in Ohio. It was published in We Make You Kindly Welcome – Recipes from The Trustees House *Daily Fare, Pleasant Hill, Kentucky by Elizabeth C. Kremer. Pleasant Hill Press, Harrodsburg, 1970.*

2 large lemons
4 eggs well beaten
2 c. sugar
1 9-inch pie shell and top crust

- Slice lemons as thin as paper, rind and all.
- Combine with sugar; mix well. Let stand 2 hours or longer, preferably blending occasionally.
- Add beaten eggs to lemon mixture; mix well.
- Turn into pie shell, arranging lemon slices evenly. Cover with the top crust. Cut several slits near the center.
- Bake at 450 degrees F. for 15 minutes. Reduce heat to 375 degrees F. and bake for about 20 minutes or until silver knife inserted near edge of pie comes out clean. Cool before serving.

BURKE'S BAKERY
Salt-Rising Bread, Gingerbread Men, & More
DANVILLE

$\mathcal{B}$urke's Bakery has been a fixture in Danville since 1934 when current baker and proprietor Joedy Burke's great grandfather brought the family business here. It moved to the Main Street location in 1942 where today passersby can get a glimpse of Burke and his staff making pies, cakes, bread, cookies, and doughnuts through the plate glass windows overlooking the sidewalk.

The bakery offers hand-made, elaborately decorated cakes for all occasions. Locals swear by the butter flake dinner rolls and the butter-top bread with its golden crust. In addition to classic glazed cake and jelly doughnuts, there's a rotating selection of specialty flavors such as strawberry, red velvet, pumpkin, and even an especially moist variety made with orange juice.

But Burke's real fame rests on two other of its specialties, one familiar and one not so much – gingerbread men and salt-rising bread.

The Burke's gingerbread men are each about the size of your hand and look, with their small heads and fat limbs, as if they were fashioned by five year olds. Don't be misled by their appearance. Heartbreakingly soft and bursting with ginger spice, they have a sophisticated flavor that puts to shame the hard, bland, mass-produced versions of the classic cookie.

Salt-rising bread is a labor-intensive loaf found in few modern bakeries, though some may offer it one or two days a week. Burke's bakes it all the time. It has its roots in early America when yeast-leavening agents were scarce. Credited as the first cookbook in the state, Mrs. Lettice Bryan's *The Kentucky Housewife* (1839) has a recipe describing the special technique of making the salt-yeast starter:

"Make a quart of water lukewarm, stir into it a table-spoonful of salt, and make a tolerably thin batter with flour; mix it well, sprinkle on the top a handful of dry flour, and set it in a warm place to rise, but be sure you do not let it get hot, or it would spoil it."

Burke's Bakery
121 Main Street
Danville, KY 40422
(859) 236-5661
www.facebook.com/pages
  /Burkes-Bakery-Delicatessen
  /104918339551300

Monday - Friday:
 7 a.m. - 6 p.m.
Saturday:
 7 a.m. - 5 p.m.
Sunday:
 12 p.m. - 4 p.m.

In short, it's tricky. So why go to the trouble?

Because salt-rising bread has a distinctive texture and tangy flavor (but flatter than sourdough's), some claim it is the best white bread ever for toasting and dressing simply with butter. A thick slice is especially appealing on a cold winter morning with a cup of dark coffee.

Finally, not the least of its virtues is that Burke's very reasonable prices seem historical, too. This may be explained by the fact that the bakery only accepts cash or checks. But the management has thoughtfully provided an ATM on the premises.

WILDERNESS TRACE DISTILLERY
Scientific Spirits
DANVILLE

ilderness Trace's name may harken back to Kentucky's pioneer history, but it is immediately apparent to visitors that the craft distillery's art is firmly rooted in 21st century science. A large whiteboard in the meeting room off of the entrance hall is covered with formulas and amino acid sequences for proteins. The first room on the tour, seen through a large window, is the distillery's laboratory where yeast strains for fermentation of vodka, rum, and bourbon are cultivated. ("Observe Scientists in Their Natural Habitat" invites a sign.) One of the distillery's founders, Pat Heist, has a Ph.D. in plant pathology.

But, as project manager Jerod Smith explains on the tour, "We have a Bluegrass fingerprint. All of our grain comes from Caverndale Farm, just three miles away." He added that this has the twin benefit of supporting the local economy and helping maintain quality control.

The distillery itself is not much bigger than the lab, though the ceiling is higher. Mash cooking, fermentation, and distilling all happen in this space. The stills were custom made for Wilderness Trace by Vendome Copper & Brass Works of Louisville, which supplies equipment to distilleries and breweries all over the world.

Next door is the milling room, where all of the grains used for the spirits are ground using the distillery's hammer mill. Some barrels are aging here as well, though Wilderness Trace is building a warehouse nearby, to which barrels will eventually be transferred and stored.

Wilderness Trace Distillery
445 Roy Arnold Avenue
Danville, KY 40422
(859) 402-8707
www.wildernesstracedistillery.com

Thursday - Friday:
  10 a.m. - 4 p.m.
Saturday:
  10 a.m. - 3 p.m.
  First and Third Saturdays,
  January - March

Tours start on the hour.

As is the case with all good tours, this one ends with a tasting and opportunity to purchase bottles. Smith pours samples of the company's Blue Heron Vodka and Harvest Rum.

Since this is Kentucky, it's not surprising that the vodka, which is 80 proof, is made with corn as well as wheat. While very clean tasting, it also exhibits a trace of corn-based sweetness, as well a hint of corn on the finish. With a smile, Smith says, "We make vodka for bourbon lovers."

The Harvest Rum (90 proof) also has both Kentucky and bourbon connections. "We made our rum from sorghum, rather than cane sugar, and source the sorghum from Townsend." (See p. 124) The rum is then aged in used bourbon barrels from Four Roses Distillery in Lawrenceburg. A very pale straw color, it has a distinctly oakier flavor than traditional dark rums.

Wilderness Trace is making bourbon, too. But good bourbon has to age longer than rum, so Smith said that the first bottling would not be until 2018. While the vast majority of bourbon produced is made by the sour mash process, whereby a little fermented mash from a previous batch is added to the next (like sourdough bread), Wilderness Road is using the sweet mash process. This differs in that each batch is totally new and contains no previously fermented grain.

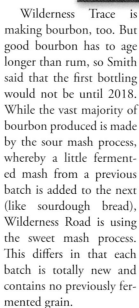

MARKSBURY FARM MARKET
Pasture-Raised Meats & More
LANCASTER

The key to the Marksbury Farm Market philosophy is its logo. Look carefully. At first glance it would seem to be just a hodgepodge of more or less vertical lines, some of which cross over others. Think about it and look again. The lines are green. The logo is stylized grass. All the meat sold in the market comes from grass-grazing animals raised in central Kentucky pastures. None of the farmers supplying meat to Marksbury uses growth hormones, antibiotics, or steroids, either.

Four business partners – cousins Preston and Greg Correll, Richard McAlister, and John-Mark Hack – opened the market and its nearby processing facility in 2010. With a variety of backgrounds in agriculture, they realized the growing "locovore" movement was creating a need for a better distribution outlet for small farmers wishing to get their products in consumers' kitchens.

Here are two tips for making the most of a visit to the market: Go at lunchtime and take a cooler.

The lunch counter offers a variety of freshly made sandwiches, including pulled pork or pimento cheese. But if you have a bigger appetite, there's a constantly changing offering of specials. In summer, look for dry-rubbed barbecued pork ribs or Jamaican jerk chicken skewers grilled on the premises. Cold weather fare may be a hearty burgoo, grilled New York strip steak, beef or chicken curry, or gyros made with slices of seasoned lamb and beef roasts.

Order lunch at the counter and then find a seat at one of the small tables inside the refurbished farmhouse or, weather permitting, on the porch or patio.

After lunch, enjoy a leisurely browse through the rooms stocked with cases of fresh meats, cheese, free-range eggs, and vegetables and the shelves stocked with all the spices and seasonings a cook would need.

The cooler will come in handy not only for the meat and produce for sale, but for quick foods such as chicken salad, house-smoked pulled pork, or smoked roast beef. Leave some room for Marksbury's popular Take-and-Bake prepared meals, too, offered on Wednesdays. Past selections have included chorizo sausage quiche, beef stroganoff, black bean and pulled pork enchiladas, and white lasagna with chicken and spinach.

Marksbury Farm Market
73 Fisher Ford Road
Lancaster, KY 40444
(859) 754-4224
www.marksburyfarm.com

Tuesday - Saturday:
 10 a.m. - 6 p.m.
  Lunch served 11 a.m. - 2 p.m.

On second thought, take two coolers.
Historical note: At the side of the road just at the entrance to Marksbury, look for a Kentucky Historical Marker. It commemorates Lancaster as the birthplace of Carry Nation, the infamous, hatchet-wielding temperance leader who was one of the most aggressive proponents of Prohibition. She was born in 1846 in a house, which still stands, about four miles from the marker's location.

So it's fitting that Lancaster is located in Garrard County, one of the 39 (out of 120) Kentucky counties that are still completely dry. No alcohol sales of any kind are permitted. Happily, Marksbury Farm Market has the Winchester-produced Ale-8-One soft drink (see p. 36) available to sip with lunch.

Pork Chops with Apple and Sage

Bone-in chops topped with the fresh combination of apples and sage, and a tangy blue cheese finishing option.

4 Marksbury pork chops
Sea salt and ground black pepper
Olive Oil
2 Granny Smith apples (unpeeled, cored and cut into 8 wedges)
1 T. of butter
A handful of fresh sage leaves
3 ½ oz. strong cheese (such as Kenny's Barren County Bleu-optional.)

- Preheat the oven to 400 degrees F. Sprinkle chops with salt and pepper.
- Coat the bottom of the pan in olive oil. Carefully brown chops for 5-6 minutes per side.
- Place on an oiled baking tray. Add apple wedges and butter to the pan and fry until lightly golden, but not soft, for 4 minutes.
- Lay 4 wedges of apple on top of each pork chop. Dress your sage leaves in a little olive oil and top each apple stack with them. Top with a small slice of cheese.
- Put the baking tray into the oven for 6 to 8 minutes until chops are fully cooked. Serve with glazed carrots and mashed potatoes.

47

BLUEBIRD CAFÉ
Organic Farm-to-Table Restaurant
STANFORD

tanford, the county seat of Lincoln County, was founded in 1775, making it one of Kentucky's oldest towns. With a population of only about 3500, you would expect Stanford to be a pretty quiet place. There is a small, handsomely restored historic district centered along Main Street with an equally handsome Beaux Arts courthouse (built 1909) topped by a clock-containing cupola. Picturesque as the town center is, it only takes about five minutes to drive through. So it would be all too easy to miss what might be Stanford's greatest asset, the Bluebird Café.

Look for the green and white awning at the corner of Main and Depot Streets. Around 8:30 a.m. on a weekday, the town center is indeed calm. Perhaps that's because most of Stanford's residents are inside the Bluebird having breakfast. Or so it seems. Every table and booth has occupants. As customers arrive or leave, wait staff greet or say good-bye to them by name.

Executive Chef William B. Hawkins and his assistants are busy in their open kitchen, where they are sautéing, flipping, toasting, grilling, griddling, and stirring up a remarkable list of dishes, all made with locally-sourced meats and produce. (Bluebird has a close partnership with Marksbury Farm Market, p. 46, among others.)

Breakfast offerings include familiar favorites such as homemade buttermilk biscuits and sausage gravy or omelets made with a choice of ingredients. Weisenberger Mills' grits are available as an a la carte option. An update on the traditional includes the Bluebird Benedict. It substitutes a fried green tomato for an English muffin and smoked Gouda cream sauce in place of the Hollandaise. French toast is made with brioche soaked in custard instead of plain egg. It may be the best French toast you'll ever eat.

The quality of the food is apparent with every bite, and with good reason.

"We do things the old way, "explains Hawkins. "I use the whole chicken to make stock." Many seasonal vegetables found on the menu come from his garden.

Hawkins had been executive chef at the prestigious Victoria National Golf Club when he saw an ad for a chef to head up a new farm-to-table restaurant

Bluebird Café
202 West Main Street
Stanford, KY 40484
(606) 365-1010
www.bluebirdnatural.com

Monday - Thursday:
 7:30 a.m. - 4 p.m.
  Breakfast served until 11 a.m.
Friday - Saturday:
 7:30 a.m. - 9 p.m.
  Dinner begins at 5 p.m.

in Stanford. His philosophy of cooking with locally-sourced, organic ingredients agreed with that of café owners Jess and Angela Correll.

"I don't know, but certainly thought, that customers would be willing to pay a little more for dishes made with these kinds of ingredients," recalls Hawkins. With a big grin he looked around the crowded restaurant, obviously pleased to know his instinct about his clientele's taste was correct.

Dynamite Chicken Salad

Lunchtime favorites include a dynamite chicken salad (Yes, it is spicy!), a fried green tomato BLT, ham and cheese sandwich in stuffed focaccia, and burgers topped with a variety of cheeses and house-made garlic aioli.

Friday and Saturday night dinner entrees change often, but there is usually a salmon dish on the menu. Since there are certainly no salmon runs in Kentucky, how does this qualify as "locally-sourced?" As it happens, Jason and Mary Beth McKinley of Wild Caught Salmon (www.wildcaughtsalmon.com) live in Stanford. Every June they go to Bristol Bay, Alaska, and catch fish which they sell year-round back in Kentucky.

The Bluebird interior and its menu are certainly sophisticated enough to be found in a much bigger city than Stanford. Asked what appealed to him about having a restaurant in such a seemingly out-of-the-way place, Hawkins had a very easy answer, "This is where the farmers are."

Not to mention the salmon fishermen.

Bluebird Chili

Chili base
2 lbs. Marksbury Farm beef
½ large yellow onion, diced
½ large red bell pepper, diced
½ large green bell pepper, diced
1 small/medium jalapeno, diced
1 T. minced garlic
1 10 oz. can diced tomato in juice
1 10 oz. can red beans
2 T. tomato paste
1 ½ c. beef broth

Seasonings
1 T. chili powder
2 t. cumin
2 t. onion powder
1 t. oregano
1 T. sugar
Salt to taste

• Brown beef, sauté onion and garlic with the beef, and drain fat.
• Add tomato paste to sautéed beef and veggies and slightly brown.
• Add dry seasonings, except sugar, and sauté another couple minutes.
• Add tomato (diced) with juice and beef broth; bring to boil and then reduce to simmer.
• Add drained and rinsed beans and sugar.
• Adjust salt, as desired.
• Simmer at least 45 minutes.
• Add tomato juice or beef broth if too thick, more tomato paste if too thin, to desired consistency.

Bon appetite!.

FOUR HILLS FARM
New American Lamb
SALVISA

When asked why he chose to raise sheep on his central Kentucky farm, Jim Mansfield, who has also farmed in New England, North Carolina, and Oklahoma, had more than one good answer. "It came to me that the land was great for forage, such as clover and alfalfa. Cattle were too big. My children were small then and I was afraid [the cattle] would hurt them – or me." Sheep just seemed to be the right animals.

But Mansfield was interested in producing meat, not wool, and he found "the perfect fit for my farm."

Katahdin sheep are an American Heritage breed developed in Maine especially for their meat. (They are named for the highest peak in the state, Mount Katahdin.) The result of crossing Caribbean-haired sheep, which are adapted to shedding their winter coats all on their own, with wooly European breeds, the Katahdin sheep don't require shearing. At the same time, they yield a mild, high quality meat.

Not only do the sheep not need shearing, their other virtues include that they feed on pasture forage, the ewes lamb outside on their own, and they are hardy enough that Mansfield doesn't need to use antibiotics or hormones to keep them healthy. He describes the meat produced from his flock of ovine paragons, "New American Lamb," since it's lean, highly nutritious due to being pasture fed, and it's excellent quality for cooking, whether grilling, roasting, or stewing.

Mansfield is something of a New American Shepherd. He used to have a herding dog, but "she passed away." He found that he could easily guide from one pasture to the next driving a four-wheel ATV. Not exactly a scene from a Thomas Hardy novel, but very efficient. Four Hills still has dogs, however.

Four Hills Farm
2471 Kirkwood Road
Salvisa, KY 40372
(859) 865-4962
www.fourhillsfarm.com

Call for an appointment.

There are no farm tours, but individuals can order and pick up cuts such as chops, shanks, legs, and whole and half lambs.

"I have four Great Pyrenees. They bond with the sheep and guard them." Mansfield said his neighbors sometimes call him when they see a dog outside the fences of the farm and think they are lost. "They're not. They live outdoors 24 hours and they are doing their job." That job is patrolling for coyotes and stray dogs that could kill or maim lambs.

And as relatively easy to care for as the Katahdin sheep are, he notes that he does have to "be here every day."

"Lambs can find more ways to get into trouble, including falling into the water tank."

Mansfield sums up his farming philosophy by saying that he worries about four things, "Caring for the livestock. Caring for the land. Producing a quality product. Making enough profit to stay in business."

Evidence that he may not need to worry too much, especially about quality, is that some of Louisville's finest restaurants, including Lilly's, Decca, Mayan Café, and Wiltshire on Market, serve his lamb.

And there's one more reason that he settled on sheep over other livestock, "I wanted to grow something I like to eat."

Four Hills Farm Lamb Stew

This came from Jim Mansfield's mother, Dorothy Rankin, who he described as a "gourmet cook."

2 Four Hills Farm Lamb Shanks
1 pinch salt & pepper (to taste)
2 T. olive oil
2 medium onions (cut vertically into wedges)
3 cloves garlic (thinly sliced)
1 small red pepper (cubed)
2 medium sweet potatoes (peeled and cut into 1-inch squares)
2 bay leaves
2 sprigs rosemary (or ½ t. dried)
1 bottle good lager beer
1 ½ c. green beans (washed and cut in half)

- Season lamb shanks generously with salt and pepper.
- Heat oil in a Dutch oven or heavy skillet over medium-high heat.
- Brown lamb on all sides. Transfer shanks to a slow cooker or crockpot.
- Add onion to pan and lightly brown for 3-4 minutes; then add red pepper and garlic slices for 2 minutes, stirring. Add to the slow cooker, along with the sweet potatoes, bay leaves, and rosemary. Salt and pepper the stew, the whole bottle of beer, and stir to mix.
- Cover and cook on low for about 5 hours.
- Add green beans for the last hour.
- When lamb is tender, remove shank bones.
- Serve hot with crusty French bread.

Serves 4-6.

LOUISVILLE REGION

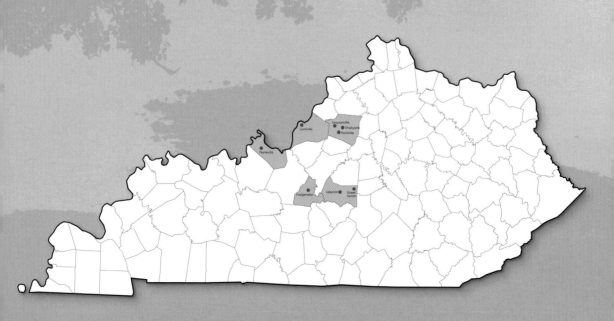

*K*entucky's largest city has a rich culinary history all its own. By some accounts, the bourbon-based Old Fashioned cocktail was first served in the bar at the private Pendennis Club in the 1880s. For today's bourbon lovers, the city has an Urban Bourbon Trail® consisting of some 30 restaurants and bars, each featuring at least 50 different bourbons (www.bourboncountry.com/things-to-do/urban-bourbon-trail/index.aspx). Beer lovers are in for a treat, too, as the list of fine local craft breweries (many of which age some of their ales and lagers in used bourbon barrels) continues to grow.

Dishes invented in the Derby City include rolled oysters, the Hot Brown, Benedictine (the cream cheese spread, not the French liqueur), Modjeska caramel candy, Henry Bain's sauce, and Derby Pie®. There is even a claim to the invention of the cheeseburger.

Kaelin's Restaurant, now closed, was a community fixture on Newberg Road in the Highlands neighborhood for decades. Soon after opening in 1934, owner Carl Kaelin made having the most flavorful hamburger in the city his culinary goal. Carl's wife Margaret was cooking a burger for him one afternoon in the restaurant's kitchen and he saw her putting away some slices of American cheese. He asked her to put one on the sizzling beef and let it melt just a bit. *Voila*, the cheeseburger was born. While there are other claims to the invention of the cheeseburger, it appeared on Kaelin's menu in October of 1934, apparently the first known printed record of the now-classic sandwich.

Of course, cheeseburgers are ubiquitous. But other Louisville dishes remain staunchly local. You'll find the best places to sample them, along with their histories, on many of the following pages.

AGAINST THE GRAIN BREWERY & SMOKEHOUSE
250 Beers in Three Years and Counting
LOUISVILLE

Two physical attributes set Against the Grain apart from other brewpubs. The first is that it is located in a graceful, 19th century redbrick building with high arched windows that once served as a train shed. The building is now the entrance to Louisville Slugger Field, home to the Louisville Bats, the AAA affiliate team to the Cincinnati Reds. The second is the three-story brew house. Visible through a glass wall behind the bar, the gleaming copper and steel fermentation tanks and brew kettles, with their network of valves and pipes, stretch from floor to ceiling, towering above the dining area.

While the name "Against the Grain" may sound rather adversarial, the business is very much a partnership, owned and operated by a quartet of beer enthusiasts – Sam Cruz, Jerry Gnagy, Andrew Ott, and Adam Watson.

"The name started as a joke," recalls Cruz, who is in charge of marketing, sales, and distribution. "Jerry and I were unloading bags of barley on a really hot day when we both worked at another brewery. It was not fun." They decided they were "against this grain" since they were so tired.

When they started ATG, they also wanted to brew differently. "All the other breweries were making the same products," said Cruz, "Brown ales, pales ales, blah, blah, blah." So Gnagy, who is the brewmaster tasked with sourcing grains and other logistics, came up with the idea to brew different beers all the time. Some sense of order is maintained since they fall into

six categories – Hop, Smoke, Dark, Malt, Session, and Whim (which obviously allows a lot of flexibility).

It's good to have these categories as a guide when ordering, since the names (often punning) tend to be colorful – Beerknuckle Bockser, Covalent Blonde, Hoppy Ending, There Gose the Neighborhood – to

**Against the Grain Brewery
& Smokehouse**
401 E. Main Street
Louisville, KY 40202
(502) 515-0174
www.atgbrewery.com

Monday - Thursday:
 11 a.m. - Midnight
  Kitchen closes at 10 p.m.
Friday - Saturday:
 11 a.m. - 2 a.m.
  Kitchen closes at 10 p.m.
Sunday:
 10 a.m. - 10 p.m.
  *Brunch Menu Exclusively
  10 a.m. - 2:30 p.m.*

name a very few. Gnagy estimates that since ATG opened in September of 2011, they have brewed more than 250 different beers. "But we reproduce some because we like them."

Daily brewing is the responsibility of Adam Watson, who patrons will see weaving his way between the fermentation tanks and brew kettles.

The ATG menu is not as endless as the beer selection, but it does have a diverse offering of dishes created to wash down with the ales and lagers. Pork risotto fritters, smoked chicken wings, and pork belly on a stick served with a side of Kentucky sorghum for dipping are among the snack bites. Order a malty pint to pair with the fine pork schnitzel sandwich dressed with house-made sauerkraut and served on a Kaiser roll. Of course, ribs, pulled pork, beef brisket, and smoked chicken are offered, too. Even beer-loving vegetarians are accommodated with a mushroom burger and a sandwich called Kentucky Fried Chiquen made with seitan.

ATG is open for lunch and dinner daily, but do be aware that parking can be a challenge on game days. The brewpub also hosts a monthly "Beer with a Scientist" evening where patrons can discuss topics from stem cells to black holes with scientists from area universities. Check the website for the schedule. No need to wear a lab coat.

Beer Can Chicken
From Chef Jordan Delewis

Whole chicken 3.5 lbs. & up
ATG Rub, ½ c. (or any seasoning of your choice)
Canola Oil, 2 T.

Beer Brine
½ gal. beer (maltly) ex. The Brown Note
½ c. kosher salt
½ c. granulated sugar
3 garlic cloves
1 sprig thyme
½ lemon

Butchers Twine

- Set your smoker or oven to 250 degrees F.
- Start by gathering all ingredients for the Beer Brine and bring to a simmer.
- Strain through a chinois/china cap and add a ½ gallon of ice to drop the temperature of the brine.
- Submerge chicken for 12 hrs. then remove, rinse under cold water & pat dry.
- Massage chicken with oil, and then sprinkle on rub of your choice.
- Smoke for about 1.5 hrs, checking on color after the first 45 minutes. If using an oven, place a pan underneath to catch drippings.
- Glaze with ATG Sauce (or your favorite BBQ sauce). OPTIONAL.
- Let rest for 30 minutes before slicing & serving.

We serve our Beer Can Chicken with cheesy Weisenberger grits & corn on the cob. Serves 4-6.

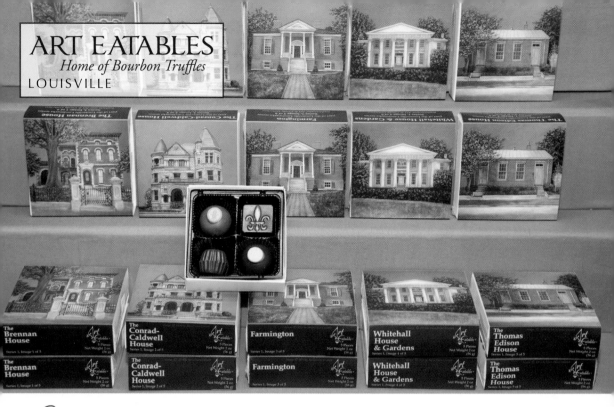

Boxes shown: The Brennan House · The Conrad-Caldwell House · Farmington · Whitehall House & Gardens · The Thomas Edison House

A rt Eatables' owner Kelly Ramsey's first career was mortgage banking, not making chocolates, except as a treat for her young son. "When you live in a cubicle, this was how to let my creativity out," she recalled one morning while she and her husband Forest prepared to open their shop.

The shelves in the small storefront located in a busy block on downtown's Fourth Street are lined with boxes of bourbon truffles. These are different from classic Kentucky bourbon balls, explained Ramsey, "A truffle has a chocolate ganache center."

Ganache is made by heating cream and pouring it over chopped chocolate, resulting in a velvety confection that dissolves in a river of flavor on the tongue. A traditional bourbon ball has a sugary center.

Ramsey uses more than 50 brands of bourbon to make her Small-Batch Bourbon Truffles™ and carefully matches her own blends of fine Belgian chocolates to the characteristic flavor profiles of each of the bourbons used. The Original Bourbon Truffle™, which helped launch the business, is made with Jim Beam White Label and milk chocolate. Denser cocoa is used for the Black Bourbon Truffle™ which plays on the darker flavor notes in Jim Beam Black, a bourbon aged twice as long (eight years) as its better known White Label sibling. Extra dark chocolate is the choice to go with Kentucky's First Truffle™ containing Evan Williams Single Barrel Vintage. The name is a nod to the claim by the bourbon's distiller, Heaven Hill, that the eponymous Williams was the state's first licensed whiskey distiller. The Louisville resident was certainly among the earliest.

Those are just three selections from among the 15 chocolates using bourbons from distilleries comprising the Kentucky Bourbon Trail®. In addition to Jim Beam and Heaven Hill, they are Four Roses, Maker's Mark, Town Branch, Wild Turkey, and Woodford Reserve. In fact, Art Eatables makes the official bourbon truffles for Maker's Mark featuring the brand's famous red star and Roman numeral logo on top of each candy.

Art Eatables
631 S. 4th Street
Louisville, KY 40202
(502) 589-0210
www.arteatables.com

Monday - Friday:
  10 a.m. - 6 p.m.
Saturday:
  10 a.m. - 5 p.m.

Distilleries from "off the trail" are showcased, too. So you'll find truffles made with Buffalo Trace's portfolio of bourbons, Jefferson's Reserve, and many of the small craft distilleries.

Ramsey says that her best selling collection in the shop is an eight-piece box from the Kentucky Bourbon Trail®. "Visitors from out of town love the idea of eating their way through the distilleries. It's a nice souvenir."

She also makes many candies featuring the fleur de lis, the symbol of the city of Louisville, and has created The Louisville Landmark Series of candies honoring several of Louisville's historic house museums. A portion of sales from these benefits the museums.

Art Eatables isn't just a hometown favorite, however. In 2014, Ramsey created 500 boxes of truffles for the guests' goodie bags at the Oscars ceremony in Los Angeles. Her candies have been featured in *Garden & Gun* Magazine and the bourbon truffles were finalists in Martha Stewart's American Made selections.

Ramsey is constantly developing candies and adding bourbons to her collection of truffles.

"Our goal is to get people to enjoy bourbon. If you give it to them in a candy, they will go try it on its own."

57

BOURBON BARREL FOODS
"Eat Your Bourbon"
LOUISVILLE

*W*hat do you get when you combine non-GMO, Kentucky-grown soybeans and red winter wheat, pure limestone spring water, a custom yeast strain, and a used bourbon barrel? You get soy sauce from the only small batch soy sauce brewery in the United States, and the only soy sauce in the world aged in bourbon barrels.

The complex, richly-flavored condiment is the flagship product of Bourbon Barrel Foods, founded in 2006 by Louisville native Matt Jamie. And like its small batch whiskey inspiration, each bottle of Bluegrass Soy Sauce is labeled with the sauce's batch and bottle number.

Jamie started Bourbon Barrel Foods with high quality spices smoked over bourbon barrel staves,

sourcing Pacific Ocean sea salt from SaltWorks in Seattle and course black pepper from India's Malabar Coast. The soy sauce was introduced in 2008 and Jamie has been adding new products ever since.

In addition to sea salt, black pepper, and a wonderfully smoky paprika, the line of seasonings now includes bourbon smoked sugar, bourbon vanilla sugar, mint julep sugar, Kentucky sorghum, vanilla extract (made with vanilla beans from Madagascar), Kentuckyaki bourbon barrel-aged teriyaki sauce, and bourbon barrel-aged Worcestershire sauce.

A few years ago Jamie developed a relationship with Woodford Reserve Distillery to use its bourbon in signature Woodford products, too. A line of mixology ingredients, including flavored bitters, simple syrups, and cocktail cherries were the result. Woodford's chef-in-residence and central Kentucky restaurateur, Ouita Michel, developed a deeply aromatic Woodford Reserve Sorghum Vinaigrette that Jamie makes and sells.

"It's been fun, but my role has changed dramatically," he recalls, explaining that he started the company as its sole operator, doing virtually everything from smoking and brewing to pasting labels on containers. In addition to making some two dozen products, he now has 15 employees and a Kitchen Studio equipped with GE Monogram® stainless steel appliances.

The kitchen is a venue for Eat Your Bourbon cooking classes where Jamie, who was a chef before he became an entrepreneur, demonstrates creative and

Bourbon Barrel Foods
Butchertown Market
1201 Story Avenue #175
Louisville, KY 40206
(502) 333-6103
www.bourbonbarrelfoods.com

Products available in the Work the Metal storefront, also located in the Butchertown Market.

Monday - Friday:
  10 a.m. - 6 p.m.
Saturday:
  10 a.m. - 5 p.m.

Bourbon Barrel Foods Retail Store
2710 Frankfort Avenue
Louisville, KY 40206
(502) 618-0939

Monday - Saturday
  10 a.m. - 6 p.m.
Sunday:
  10 a.m. - 4 p.m.

delicious ways to incorporate his products in recipes. (Participants dine on the results.) It also hosts guest chefs from around the city and even throughout the South, including a recent visit by Sean Brock of Charleston, who also signed copies of his new cookbook, *Heritage*. Brock has used Bourbon Barrel Foods' products in many of his dishes, including teriyaki sauce for Kentuckyaki glazed pig ear lettuce wraps with sweet marinated cucumbers at his restaurant, Husk.

Since its founding, Bourbon Barrel Foods has been located in a converted warehouse space in Louisville's historic Butchertown neighborhood, where there is room to smoke sugars and spices and store barrels of aging sauces. The products can be found in most area groceries and are sold nationally through Williams-Sonoma, Whole Foods, and other gourmet retailers. In January 2015, Bourbon Barrel Foods finally got its own storefront at 2710 Frankfort Avenue.

When asked if he saw any limits to his company's growth, Jamie had a quick response. "It's harder now to get barrels."

Repurposed bourbon barrels are being used by brewers around the country in which to age and flavor craft beers. And Jamie isn't the only specialty food maker using the charred, whiskey-soaked containers. He noted that, "Some people in Brooklyn are aging pickles in bourbon barrels."

BBF Pimento Cheese
Pimento cheese is also known as "The Caviar of the South" and Bourbon Barrel Foods' ingredients make an especially spicy version of this traditional spread.

1 ½ c. mayonnaise
1 (4oz.) jar of diced pimentos, drained
1 t. Bourbon Barrel Aged Worcestershire Sauce
¼ t. Bourbon Barrel Smoked Paprika
1 t. finely grated red onion
¼ t. ground Bourbon Barrel Smoked Pepper
1 (8 oz.) block of extra-sharp Cheddar cheese, finely shredded
1 (8 oz.) block of white Cheddar cheese, finely shredded

• In a large bowl, stir the first five ingredients. Then stir in the cheese.
• Serve with crackers, pretzels, or bread. Keep refrigerated up to a week.

59

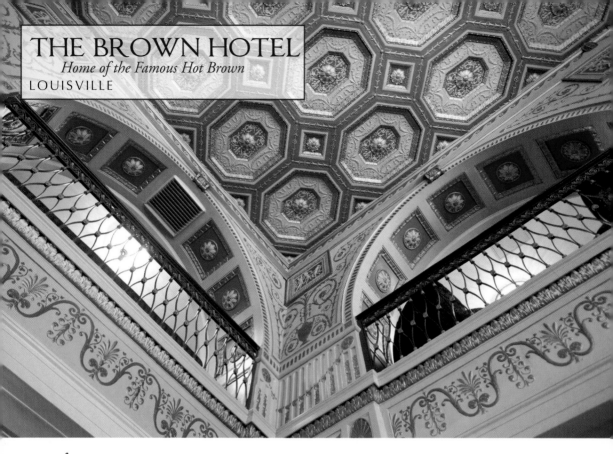

THE BROWN HOTEL
Home of the Famous Hot Brown
LOUISVILLE

*I*n his compendium of regional foods, *Southern Belly*, John T. Edge perfectly captures the sensations attendant to eating what has become Louisville's signature dish, the Hot Brown:

"On a recent Saturday morning, I took a seat in the hotel's J. Graham's Restaurant and sank into an overstuffed chair to await my prize. In short order it arrived in a brown faux skillet made of crockery, trailing scents of toasted cheese and fried bacon. The Mornay sauce was still burbling when my waiter presented the dish with a flourish. One forkful and I knew I was in the presence of something special, a dish unparalleled in its richness, its reckless disregard for dietary restraint. Within moments I was wiping the last bits of Mornay from the skillet with a toast point. Two cups of hot coffee later I was able to clamber to my feet, sated but woozy, drunk on cholesterol and calories."

What Edge relished for breakfast actually began as a late night snack for guests dancing in the Brown Hotel's ballroom. The opulent Brown opened in 1923 and was the venue for many high society parties and weddings. It also hosted nightly dinner dances lasting into the wee hours. When dancers needed a break, they would go to the hotel's restaurant for a restorative meal.

The Brown Hotel
335 W. Broadway
Louisville, KY 40202
(502) 583-1234
www.brownhotel.com

J. Graham's Café
  Daily:
    7 a.m. - 3 p.m.

The English Grill
  Monday - Thursday:
    6 p.m. - 9 p.m.
  Friday - Saturday:
    5 p.m. - 10 p.m.

The Lobby Bar
  Daily:
    3 p.m. - 1:30 a.m.

One night in 1926, Chef Fred Schmidt decided he'd had enough of slinging ham and eggs and vowed to create something new and different. He constructed an open-faced sandwich with sliced turkey smothered in creamy Mornay sauce, topped it with bacon for color, and finished it with a pinch of seasoning. He then popped the whole thing under the broiler until the cheese was brown and bubbly. In essence, a hybrid sandwich/casserole, the Hot Brown has been a staple of the hotel restaurants' menus ever since. And while many other Kentucky restaurants have tried to copy it (often with their own variations on the theme), the definitive version is still the one found here.

Whether you order it in the casual J. Graham's Café, the white tablecloth English Grill, or the comfortable Lobby Bar, the Hot Brown will not disappoint. The hotel is a member of the Urban Bourbon Trail, and a shot of bourbon pairs splendidly with a late night Hot Brown. Just the thing if you are staying at the Brown, which is one of the Historic Hotels of America designated by the National Trust for Historic Preservation, and a AAA Four Diamond hotel.

The Hot Brown

1 ½ T. salted butter
1 ½ T. all-purpose flour
1 ½ c. heavy cream
¼ c. Pecorino Romano cheese, plus extra for garnish
Pinch of ground nutmeg
Salt and pepper
14 oz. sliced roasted turkey breast, sliced thick
4 slices of Texas toast (crusts trimmed)
4 slices of bacon
2 Roma tomatoes, sliced in half
Paprika
Parsley

- In a two-quart saucepan, melt butter and slowly whisk in flour until combined to form a thick paste or roux. Continue to cook roux for 2 minutes over medium-low heat, stirring frequently. Whisk heavy cream into the roux and cook over medium heat until the cream begins to simmer, about 2-3 minutes. Remove sauce from heat and slowly whisk in Pecorino Romano cheese until the Mornay sauce is smooth. Add nutmeg, salt and pepper to taste.
- For each Hot Brown, place one slice of toast in an oven-safe dish and cover with 7 oz. of turkey. Take the two halves of the Roma tomato and two toast points and set them alongside the base of turkey and toast. Pour half of the sauce over the dish, completely covering it. Sprinkle with additional cheese. Place entire dish under a broiler until cheese begins to brown and bubble. Remove and cross two pieces of crispy bacon on top. Sprinkle with paprika and parsley and serve immediately.

Makes two sandwiches.

CELLAR DOOR CHOCOLATES
Updated Bourbon Balls and More
LOUISVILLE

*E*rika Chavez-Graziano and her team of creative chocolatiers fashion such utterly charming candies – chocolate frogs for Harry Potter fans, zombie bunnies at Halloween, jockey silks lollies for Derby, marshmallow snowmen at Christmas – you almost hate to eat them. Almost.

The shop also stocks artisanal toffees, fudge, barks and bars, brittles, and caramels. And then, there are the bourbon balls.

Made with Evan Williams bourbon distilled in Louisville, the candies give off multi-colored shimmers from the 16- and 32-piece Bourbon Ball Museum Boxes. These are not your grandfather's bourbon balls. In addition to the classic version, the collection contains sorghum, maple, honey, vanilla, pumpkin, bourbon and Coke, dark chocolate, baked apple, brown butter, brown sugar, mint julep, dulce, cherry cordial, espresso, and pecan variations on the bourbon ball theme.

"The colors come from natural food dyes we put in cocoa butter that lines the molds into which we pour the chocolate," Chavez-Graziano explains. This also gives her candies a beautiful sheen, as if they have been polished.

Indeed, you are tempted to shield your eyes during a visit to the Cellar Door Chocolates shop in the Butcher-town Market, with its gleaming glass cases filled with row upon row of colorful confections and dark wood shelves lined

with jars of jelly beans, truffles, chocolate covered pretzels, and a selection of whimsical candies that include addictive pale green "olives" made of white chocolate surrounding a roasted almond center. (Do not drop these into a martini. But they are delicious as an accompaniment while sipping one!)

Chavez-Graziano started her business in 2007, after realizing that she was bored with her master's thesis. Her real passion was making chocolates and her friends urged her to turn that enthusiasm into a business. She began by making confections to sell wholesale, but soon people who had tasted them wanted to buy them directly and the retail shop followed.

Cellar Door Chocolates
Butchertown Market
1201 Story Avenue #109
Louisville, KY 40206
(502) 561-2940
www.cellardoorchocolates.com

Monday - Friday:
 10 a.m. - 6 p.m.
Saturday:
 10 a.m. - 5 p.m.

In addition to the Museum Collection, an array of bourbon buttercreams are made using several different whiskeys, including Old Forester, Michter's, Knob Creek, Buffalo Trace, Four Roses, and Elijah Craig. Interestingly, these sweet treats, while extremely popular, are not Cellar Door's biggest seller.

"Our most popular [candies] are the sea salt caramels," Chavez-Graziano said, which has inspired a new project for Cellar Door. Plans are in the works to open a storefront that will offer tastings of a variety caramels and chocolates with bourbons.

Meanwhile, Cellar Door has many other distinctions. It provided candy as a sponsor for the 2014 Emmy Awards in Los Angeles, provides chocolates for the Kentucky Derby Festival and Actors Theatre of Louisville, and is the only chocolatier in Kentucky to use Fortunato No. 4 chocolate from Peru, into which it makes a remarkably rich and complex dark chocolate bar.

Even if you can't make it to the Louisville shop, you can still enjoy the bounty from Cellar Door via its Gourmet Chocolate Club, delivering chocolate to your door. One month, six month, and yearlong memberships are available. Selections are seasonal. So, for example, expect a bourbon ball bounty in May, the month in which the Kentucky Derby is held.

CHECK'S CAFÉ
Preserving the Rolled Oyster Tradition
LOUISVILLE

Greg Haner, the fourth-generation proprietor of the Mazzoni's Café, which opened its doors in downtown Louisville in 1884, was quoted in *The Louisville Encyclopedia* about his family's most famous dish, "[A rolled oyster] is three or four oysters dipped in batter, and formed in more cracker meal. As you deep fry them the outside gets golden brown and the oysters on the inside steam and burst. Their liquor goes all through the dough on the inside, making it all taste like oyster. It's something different, it's indigenous to Louisville as far as we know, and we've been doing it the longest."

In fact, Mazzoni's served rolled oysters throughout a migration of locations, for 125 years, until the last incarnation of the restaurant closed in 2009. The dish started out as a free snack to drinkers at the original saloon. When Prohibition arrived, the snack became a menu staple.

While Mazzoni's is gone, the rolled oyster lives on. It does so most traditionally at another neighborhood, family-owned operation, Check's Café.

Check's "only" dates to 1944, having opened for business the year "Casablanca" won the Oscar for Best Picture and Bing Crosby and the Andrews Sisters had a number one hit single with Cole Porter's "Don't Fence Me In." John Murrow, the grandson of the original proprietors, Joe and Mary Murrow, now oversees daily operations.

Located in the historically working class Germantown/Schitzelberg neighborhood of tidy shotgun houses, Check's has long enjoyed a reputation for good food at extremely reasonable prices. As of this writing, the most expensive dish on the menu is fried chicken, at $7.50. Everything else is under $7. At lunchtime, the café attracts not only the neighborhood regulars, but also busy professionals from nearby Downtown and the occasional tourist in pursuit of authentic local color.

In addition to the rolled oysters, other top sellers are the out-sized

Check's Café
1101 E. Burnett Avenue
Louisville, KY 40217
(502) 637-9515
www.checkscafe.com

Monday - Thursday:
  11 a.m. - 11 p.m.
Friday:
  11 a.m. - Midnight
Saturday:
  11 a.m. - 1 a.m.
Sunday:
  1 p.m. - 10 p.m.

fried fish sandwich and the bratwurst, both served on rye. The Braunschweiger sandwich is popular, too. (This is Germantown, after all.) Locally brewed Falls City Beer (a very tasty pale ale) is served on tap and highly recommended as an accompaniment to the favorites.

If you visit, do be aware of the rather unusual ordering etiquette. A line forms by the cash register at the bar. This is where you place your order. But you do not give your name. Repair to your table with your drink and listen for your order to be called, as in "rolled oyster and onion rings" or "fish sandwich and German potato salad."

Believe it or not, this works remarkably well.

Rolled Oysters
This recipe from Saveur, *5 January, 2009.*

1 c. white cornmeal
½ c. flour
1 t. baking powder
½ t. kosher salt
⅓ c. milk
18 medium oysters, such as bluepoints, shucked (about ½ lb.)
2 T. of the liquor reserved
1 egg, beaten
Canola oil, for frying
Tartar sauce or ketchup (or cocktail sauce), for serving

• Put cornmeal into a shallow dish and set aside. Over a large bowl, sift together the flour, baking powder, and salt. Stir in the milk, reserved oyster liquor, and egg. Add oysters to the batter and toss to coat. Using one hand, scoop out 3 oysters and roll in cornmeal, forming a patty. Transfer oyster patty to a parchment paper–lined baking sheet and repeat with remaining oysters.

• Pour canola oil into a 12" cast-iron skillet so that it reaches a depth of 1". Heat skillet over medium-high heat until a deep-fry thermometer registers 350 degrees F. Fry the oyster patties in batches, turning occasionally with a slotted spoon, until golden brown, 3–4 minutes. Transfer to a paper towel–lined plate. Repeat with remaining oyster patties; serve with tartar sauce, cocktail sauce, or ketchup.

Makes 6 rolled oysters.

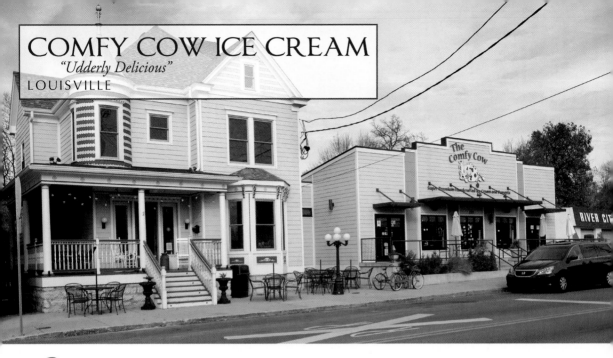

COMFY COW ICE CREAM
"Udderly Delicious"
LOUISVILLE

Seekers of seriously good ice cream will have no trouble spotting the Comfy Cow building on Frankfort Avenue in Crescent Hill. It's the only turreted Victorian house painted hot pink, as is the modern storefront connected to it. Plus, there's a neon ice cream cone in the window.

Inside, patrons will find not only dozens of flavors of ice cream made with high quality ingredients, they can also choose from a variety of decadent treats from chocolate- or sprinkle-dipped frozen bananas, ice cream pies and ice cream sandwiches, and enormous, multi-ingredient ice cream sundaes. After ordering at the counter, patrons can take their frozen goodies to a table in the restored 19th century house connected to the shop decorated with vintage record covers, second hand furniture, and cow memorabilia. (Where *did* the owners find that string of little cow Christmas tree lights?)

The Cow has quickly become a local institution, but it hasn't been around all that long.

By the late 2000s, owners Tim and Roy Koons-Magee were ready for career changes. Having made livings in construction and health care respectively, they each wanted to try something new and something they could do together. After considering several possible businesses, they decided that Louisville needed a gourmet ice cream shop and the first Comfy Cow starting scooping on December 1, 2009.

Open an ice cream shop in winter?

According to Tim Koons-Magee, "We had been trying for months and months to acquire financing and as you probably recall, it was the height of the 'Great Recession'. When we finally got a yes (after about 10 or 11 months), their terms were such that we would need to take the money and so the prover-

bial clock starting ticking. As it turned out, we were fortunate in being able to have a few months to iron out the wrinkles before the onslaught that ensued beginning in the spring."

Sixteen signature flavors are available year-round, including Cow Tracks, a rich peanut butter and chocolate collaboration. Seasonal flavors change every month. In an ideal world, the citrusy Lemon Crunch and spicy Mexican Chocolate would be available at the same time. But with enough forethought (and a lot of self control), it is possible to stockpile cartons in your home freezer.

When asked which were the bestselling flavors, Tim Koons-Magee replied, "Believe it or not it is some of the more traditional flavors like Cookies and Cream, Cookie Monster Dough, Vanilla, and Chocolate."

Comfy Cow Ice Cream
2221 Frankfort Avenue
Louisville, KY 40206
(502) 409-4616
www.thecomfycow.com

Sunday - Thursday:
  11 a.m. - 10 p.m.
Friday - Saturday:
  11 a.m. - 11 p.m.

Other Locations
Westport Village
1301 Herr Lane
Louisville, KY 40222
(502) 425-4979

Sunday - Thursday:
  11 a.m. - 10 p.m.
Friday - Saturday:
  11 a.m. - 11 p.m.

339 Cardinal Boulevard
Louisville, KY 40208
(502) 409-5090

Daily:
  12 p.m. - 11 p.m.

1449 Bardstown Road
Louisville, KY 40204

Sunday - Thursday:
  11 a.m. - 10 p.m.
Friday - Saturday:
  11 a.m. - 11 p.m.

Currently, there are four Cow locations in Louisville and one across the river in New Albany, Indiana. Franchise opportunities may mean more stores opening in the future. And several area restaurants serve ice cream customized by Comfy Cow to fit their menus.

Naturally, the shops attract lots of families with children. But there are some decidedly adult treats, too. Considering that the growing herd of Comfy Cows is Louisville-based, it is not surprising that two of the signature flavors feature Old Forester bourbon. Georgia butter pecan Simply Southern is infused with bourbon and loaded with pecan pie pieces and dark chocolate chips. Bourbon Ball is a luscious vanilla with chocolate chip ice cream, also infused with the Louisville-made bourbon.

The good news for ice cream addicts who don't live in Louisville is that pints and quarts of Comfy Cow can be ordered online and shipped throughout the country. Check the website for details.

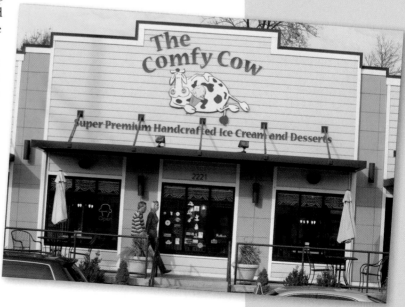

DISTILLED SPIRITS EPICENTER
Distilling School at Moonshine University
LOUISVILLE

*I*t's nine o'clock on a sunny May morning and class is about to start for a roomful of students just finishing coffee, fresh fruit, and pastries. Seats are taken at tables arranged in long rows facing the front of the room where instructors Kevin Hall (Operations Manager) and Colin Blake (Headmaster of Liquorial Studies) are retrieving their PowerPoint lecture slides. They begin class by asking each of the participants to introduce themselves. Then the first slide appears on the screen:

"DISCLAIMER: It is *illegal* to distill alcohol without a permit."

Thus begins class for the one-day Bourbon Making Workshop at Moonshine University.

Housed in the Distilled Spirits Epicenter, Moonshine University is the school for both individuals interested in opening craft distilleries and spirits enthusiasts who simply want to learn the details of milling, fermenting, and distilling grain into alcohol. In addition to bourbon, other classes teach about making rye, gin, vodka, and even absinthe. The classes for aspiring professionals typically last for five days and the school calls on a team of more than 30 experts, from historians to mixologists, to teach.

Today's workshop starts with definitions of whiskey in general and bourbon in particular. "Whiskey," Hall explains, "must be made from fermented grain, distilled no higher than 190 proof, put into an oak container, and bottled at no less than 80 proof."

Blake clarifies that bourbon is a type of whiskey, just as is rye or Scotch.

"Bourbon has to have 51% corn in the mash bill. It must be made in the USA. It must come off the still at less than 160 proof and cut to less than 125 proof (with distilled water) before barreling. And it must be put in a new, charred oak container."

Distilled Spirits Epicenter
801 S. Eighth Street
Louisville, KY 40203
(502) 301-8126
www.ds-epicenter.com

*Hours vary depending upon class
schedules.*

The lecture then turns distilling terminology and chemistry before students move into the "lab" – the Grease Monkey Distillery – for their practicum. (The space was formerly an auto repair shop, hence the name.) This is the hands-on part of the workshop where everyone takes turns with tasks from filling the cooker with milled grain to testing the distillate that comes off the still.

Vendome Copper & Brass Works, a family-owned maker of fermentation and distilling equipment that has been manufacturing stills in Louisville for more than a century, made the equipment in the artisan distillery. Hall told the class that Vendome donated the 250-gallon distilling system since Grease Monkey doubles as the manufacturer's showroom. Most American whiskey is made in column stills and most Scottish whiskey in pot stills. Grease Monkey has a custom-made hybrid still that can be used to make a variety of spirits.

The class breaks for a catered lunch before the afternoon's sensory portion of the class. Blake and Hall talk about the importance of aging in charred barrels and students compare the color and flavor profiles of four bourbons: Old Forester (86 proof), Old Forester Signature (100 proof), Maker's Mark (90 proof), and Maker's 46 (also 90 proof, but extra-aged with charred oak staves).

The class wraps up with discussion of the flavors often found in bourbons. Most of today's students were from the Louisville area, but the school attracts participants from around the country and the world.

"We've had people from almost 40 states and five or six countries," says Hall, "including Kazakhstan and Vietnam."

69

GEORGE GAGEL TRUCK FARM
Growing Authentic Limestome Bibb Lettuce
LOUISVILLE

With his infectious smile and engaging, easy-going manner, you would never suspect that George Gagel has inherited a serious responsibility. He is the keeper of a rare horticultural heritage.

"Ours is the only greenhouse I know of that grows Limestone Bibb from the original seed strain," Gagel says proudly one frosty fall morning at the beginning of lettuce growing session.

John B. Bibb developed this unique variety of lettuce in the garden of his Frankfort, Kentucky, home at 411 Wapping Street around 1865. (The 20-room house is still a private residence.) Bibb, who had served as an officer in the Civil War, as well as a Kentucky State Representative and Senator, was an amateur horticulturalist. He developed the lettuce he named after the limestone soil in which he cultivated it by crossing spinach and a lettuce variety now lost to history. The result was a buttery-tender, richly flavored lettuce that grows in deep green rosettes about the size of a woman's fist.

Seeds from Bibb's garden made it to Louisville via his maid, who was friends with Viola Genenwein, whose brother William was a vegetable grower in the city. He and colleague Stanley Siewart starting selling the lettuce

commercially to high-end restaurants in Louisville and Chicago, actually driving the produce north themselves, since lettuce shipped by train wilted.

Eventually, through a series of grower exchanges, Bibb seeds came to the Gagel family in the mid-1960s, a century since John Bibb had developed it.

Today, George Gagel grows many varieties of vegetables, flowers, and ferns on his ten and a half acre farm surrounded by Louisville's southwestern suburbs. The fourth generation operation is doing well. The Agribusiness Industry Network named it "Agribusiness of the Year" for the Kentuckiana region in 2014.

As the summer growing season starts winding down, Gagel turns his attention to Bibb lettuce,

George Gagel Truck Farm
2400 Lower Hunters Trace
Louisville, KY 40216
(502) 447-6809

Mid-March - August 31
Monday - Saturday:
8 a.m. - 6 p.m.

September 1 - Mid-March
Hours are seasonal. Please call.

which is nurtured inside the 100,000 square feet of greenhouses. Tiny seeds, about the size of very slender rice grains, are sown in flats. Once the plants are large enough, they are transferred to the soil in the greenhouses where they grow until big enough to harvest. Available until May, Limestone Bibb can be purchased at the farm's store. A local distributor, Creation Gardens, also provides it to area groceries and restaurants. So if you see Bibb salad on a menu, be sure to ask where the restaurant gets its produce.

"With hydroponic Bibb, you don't get the true flavor," says Gagel. "It's tissue paper."

He's absolutely right.

A Simple Limestone Bibb Lettuce Salad
Bibb lettuce is so flavorful that it does not need a lot of dressing.

Use 1 small head Limestone Bibb per person.
For each:
6 slices ripe avocado
1 T. sliced toasted almonds
½ t. coarsely ground black pepper (Bourbon Barrel Foods' is terrific.)
1 t. high quality extra virgin olive oil
¼ t. fresh lemon juice

• Separate all of the leaves from the lettuce head and arrange in concentric layers on a salad plate.
• Arrange avocado slices in a pinwheel pattern.
• Sprinkle with almonds and pepper.
• Drizzle with oil and lemon juice and serve.

71

LILLY'S – A KENTUCKY BISTRO
Louisville's Original Farm-to-Table Restaurant

LOUISVILLE

It's a firmly established trend now, but when chef/owner Kathy Cary opened Lilly's (named after her daughter) more than a quarter century ago, she was Louisville's farm-to-table pioneer. Having grown up on a Kentucky farm with chickens and cattle and where her parents gardened and cooked with their own vegetables, Cary was receptive when a young farming couple showed up at her restaurant's doorstep in the early 1990s.

"They wanted to sell me everything they had and I bought it. Afterwards they'd go to the movies," recalls Cary with a laugh. Cary and the couple from Hart County settled into a routine where she would call in an order for herbs, greens, tomatoes, blueberries, peppers, eggplant and whatever else might be in season on Tuesday, and they would deliver the produce on Thursday. "They are my barefoot hippie farmers." But they aren't her only farmers.

A list on the back of Lilly's seasonally changing menu – often described as "Southern with a twist" – features more than two dozen local producers and suppliers, not only farmers (vegetables, fruit, meat, fish), but wineries and distilleries. (The restaurant is a stop on Louisville's Urban Bourbon Trail.)

Cary uses locally-raised Amish chicken in her signature chicken pot pie, a rosemary-scented delight

with a flakey crust featured as a lunch menu staple for many years. Today it anchors the menu in Cary's adjacent gourmet-to-go shop, La Peche.

A dinner entrée that appears from time to time is one Cary describes as "Using the whole animal, right there on the plate." The Stone Cross Farms' Seven Deadly Sins features pork tenderloin with Angel's Envy bourbon cream sauce (above), pork belly, bacon-infused macaroni and cheese, bahn mi egg roll, jowl bacon collards, sliced cured ham, and crispy ear crackling with blackberry sauce.

Other meaty treats usually found on the Lilly's menu are veal scaloppine (sauces change) and the Old Hat Cattle Company burger. But vegetarians are accommodated, too. Look for a Farmers' Vegetable Plate, as well as seasonally changing vegetarian pasta.

Cary's farm fresh creativity is served in a series of intimate dining rooms by knowledgeable and friendly staff. Pastoral murals grace some walls. One is a copy of the famous Howard Chandler Christy wood nymphs from Manhattan's Café Des Artistes. Another is a farm scene that seems part Kentucky, part Provence. Other rooms feature paintings and multimedia works by local artists.

Kathy Cary is no doubt one of Kentucky's leading chefs. But her reputation extends well beyond the

Lilly's – A Kentucky Bistro
1147 Bardstown Road
Louisville, KY 40204
(502) 451-0447
www.lillysbistro.com

Tuesday - Saturday:
 Lunch, 11 a.m. - 3 p.m.
 Dinner, 5 p.m. - 10 p.m.

Bluegrass State. Her restaurant and recipes have been featured in numerous national food publications and Cary is the most-nominated chef from Kentucky for the James Beard Awards. She was the first from the state to cook at the famed Beard House in New York City.

But Cary doesn't rest on her excellent reputation. She's always looking for new flavors and new ways to use the best products. She leads food tours to Europe, South America, and even Eastern Kentucky, where she says her world traveler guests are delighted by "the unexpected." The tours sell out almost instantly.

Saturday is about the only morning you won't find Cary making soups, pot pies, and stock in Lilly's kitchen. That's when she scouts the aisles of the city's farmers' markets. "How rich the state is with our farmers!"

Not to mention how rich with the chefs, like Kathy Cary, who champion them.

Kathy Cary's Original Chicken Pot Pie
This rich, savory, pot pie graced the cover of the February 2001 issue of Bon Appétit.

Crust
2 ½ c. all purpose flour
½ t. salt
1 c. (2 sticks) unsalted butter, cut into pieces, room temperature
1 8 oz. package cream cheese, cut into pieces, room temperature

- Mix flour and salt in processor. Add butter and cheese; blend until moist clumps form.
- Shape dough into 6-inch long log.
- Wrap and chill while making chicken and the filling.

Chicken
1-3 ½ lbs. whole chicken
12 c. water
2 large onions, quartered
2 large carrots, coarsely chopped
1 large leek, sliced
12 small thyme sprigs
1 bay leaf

- Place all ingredients in a large pot; bring to boil. Reduce heat; simmer until chicken is cooked through, about 45 minutes.
- Transfer chicken to a large bowl; cool. Discard skin and bones.
- Cut meat into 1-inch pieces; return to bowl. Strain cooking liquid into large saucepan. Boil until reduced to 3 cups stock, about 1 hour.

Filling and Assembly
3 T. olive oil
2 red bell peppers, cut into strips

1 large onion, chopped
8 oz. shiitake mushrooms, stemmed, caps sliced
4 oz. green beans, boiled 1 minute, cut into 1-inch pieces
¾ c. chopped green onions
½ c. drained oil-packed sun-dried tomatoes, chopped
1 T. chopped rosemary
½ c. (1 stick) unsalted butter
½ c. plus 2 T. all-purpose flour
1 c. milk
¼ c. whipping cream
4 ½ t. beef base or other concentrated beef-flavored broth
1 egg, beaten (for glaze)

- Heat 1 tablespoon of oil in a large skillet over medium heat. Add peppers and onion; cook until soft, about 6 minutes. Transfer to bowl with chicken. Heat 2 tablespoons oil in same skillet over medium-high heat. Add mushrooms; sauté until just brown, about 4 minutes. Add to bowl with chicken. Mix in next 4 ingredients.
- Melt butter in a large saucepan over medium heat. Add flour; whisk 2 minutes. Gradually whisk in 3 cups stock, then milk, cream, and beef base; bring to boil. Season sauce with salt and pepper. Stir 3 cups sauce into chicken mixture (reserve remaining sauce for another use).
- Cut prepared dough crosswise into 6 equal pieces. Roll out pieces to 7-inch rounds on lightly floured surface. Divide filling among six 2-cup soufflé dishes. Cover each dish with 1 dough round. Press overhang to side of dish to adhere. (Can be made one day ahead. Cover; chill.)
- Preheat oven to 350 degrees F. Brush top of each dough round with egg glaze; cut 3 slits in each for steam to escape. Bake pies until crust is golden brown and filling is heated through, about 45 minutes.

Makes 6.

NULU
East Market Street Restaurant, Shopping, and Gallery District
LOUISVILLE

*L*ouisville has an impressive selection of restaurants and creative chefs. During the 1980s and 1990s, creative new eateries sprang up along what became Restaurant Rows along Bardstown Road in the Highlands neighborhood and Frankfort Avenue in Crescent Hill/Clifton. The latest dining district to emerge has been NuLu (for "New Louisville"), a four-block-long area on the East Market and East Main Streets corridor of downtown. There are more than a dozen restaurants and taprooms, an equal number of art galleries and theaters, and almost two dozen boutique shops ranging from gardening accessories to antiques.

There's even installation art at one of the restaurants. **The Garage Bar** at the corner of Market and Clay is very easy to spot. It's in the building with the very, very slow car crash out front. Two vehicles on conveyors confront one another in a glacially-paced head-on collision. When their hoods are completely collapsed, the cars are swapped out for new ones. The restaurant, which specializes in wood oven-fired pizzas, is housed in a former auto repair shop and large bay doors open onto the large patio in good weather. Don't miss a gin and tonic made with the house-made tonic. It goes great with a selection of raw oysters or the country ham tasting flight. (www.garageonmarket.com)

Harvest, one of the city's premiere farm-to-table restaurants, is located in the 600 block of East Market. Local farmers are celebrated as heroes with five-foot high black-and-white photos of each lining the walls. Chef Coby Ming's specialties include buttermilk fried chicken with peppercorn gravy and a smoked pork chop with succotash. Dishes change seasonally, too. Harvest is also one of the members of the Urban Bourbon Trail and serves an excellent Old Fashioned made with locally produced bitters. (www.harvestlouisville.com)

Just a couple of doors down, you'll find the intimate, eclectic **Wiltshire on Market.** Share the charcuterie and cheese board with grilled bread to start, and enjoy the works of local artists that decorate the space. Weather-permitting, reserve a table on the tiny, walled patio garden. The menu of delectable contemporary American fare, including truly gourmet vegetarian dishes (eggplant and zucchini Napoleon with goat cheese, sun-dried tomato, and toasted quinoa for example) changes weekly. (wiltshirepantry.com/wiltshire-on-market/)

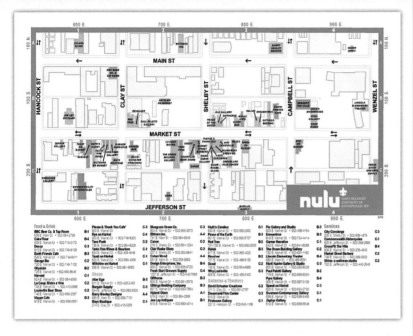

MAIN ST

CLAY ST

SHELBY ST

CAMPBELL ST

WENZEL ST

HANCOCK ST

MARKET ST

JEFFERSON ST

nulu EAST MARKET DISTRICT IN LOUISVILLE, KY

Food & Drink
BBC Beer Co. & Tap Room — B-1
636 E. Main St. • 502-384-2739
Cake Flour — C-2
909 E. Market St. • 502-719-0172
Decca — C-3
812 E. Market St. • 502-749-8128
Earth Friends Cafe — C-1
631 E. Market St. • 502-749-6911
Garage Bar — C-1
700 E. Market St. • 502-749-7100
Ghyslain — C-2
721 E. Market St. • 502-690-8646
Harvest — C-1
624 E. Market St. • 502-384-9090
La Coop: Bistro a Vins — C-2
732 E. Market St. • 502-410-2988
Louisville Beer Store — C-2
746 E. Market St. • 502-569-2337
Mayan Cafe — C-3
813 E. Market St. • 502-566-0651
Please & Thank You Cafe' — C-3
800 E. Market St.
Rye on Market — B-4
900 E. Market St. • 502-749-6200
Taco Punk — C-3
726 S. Market St. • 502-384-6028
Taste Fine Wines & Bourbon — B-3
634 E. Market St. • 502-409-4646
Toast on Market — B-2
620 E. Market St. • 502-569-4099
Wiltshire on Market — C-2
636 E. Market St. • 502-681-8760

Shops
Alter Ego — C-2
611 E. Market St. • 502-426-2495
Bargain Supply — C-2
644 E. Jefferson St. • 502-582-6000
Barry Wooley Designs — B-3
635 E. Main St. • 502-568-7101
Bays Boutique
214 S. Clay St. • 502-419-0285

Bluegrass Green Co. — C-3
604 E. Market St. • 502-365-3573
Blithers Inc. — C-4
731 E. Main St. • 502-584-6349
Canoe — C-3
216 S. Shelby St. • 502-561-1234
Clair Ruabe Glass — C-3
207 S. Shelby St. • 502-292-6841
Cohen Wood — C-4
721 E. Main St. • 502-653-9663
Design Enterprises, Inc. — B-4
908 E. Market St. • 502-583-9720
Fresh Start Growers' Supply — B-4
1007 E. Jefferson St. • 502-442-7883

Gittings Bedding Company
807 E. Market St. • 502-583-7954
Hyland Glass — B-3
619 E. Main St. • 502-384-2689
Joe Ley Antiques — B-1
615 E. Market St. • 502-583-4014

Muth's Candies — C-3
630 E. Market St. • 502-585-2952
Peace of the Earth — A-4
801 E. Market St. • 502-690-5707
Red Tree — C-2
701-705 E. Market St. • 502-582-2635
Relish — C-3
207 S. Shelby St. • 502-365-4222
Revolver — A-4
707 E. Market St. • 502-456-6130
Scout — B-4
742 E. Market St. • 502-584-8988
Why Louisville — A-4
614 E. Market St. • 502-456-5400

Galleries & Theaters
David Schuster Creations — C-2
910 E. Market St. • 502-561-2787
Dreamland Film Center — C-3
810 E. Market St.
Firehouse Gallery — B-1
221 S. Hancock St. • 502-640-1169

Flo Gallery and Studio — C-1
605 E. Market St. • 502-456-4154
Encounters — B-3
601 E. Market St. • 502-724-4474
Gunner Narrative — C-1
642 E. Market St. • 502-814-8096
The Green Building Gallery — B-3
732 E. Market St. • 502-565-1162
Lincoln Elementary Theater — B-4
926 E. Main St. • 502-485-8091
Murti Kashin Gallery & Studio — C-1
800 E. Market St. • 502-290-6029
Paul Paletti Gallery — C-1
713 E. Market St. • 502-589-9254
Pyro Gallery — B-4
909 E. Market St. • 502-587-0106
Speed on Market — C-2
814 E. Market St. • 502-634-2700
Swanson Contemporary Gallery — C-1
638 E. Market St.
Zephyr Gallery — C-1
610 E. Market St. • 502-608-8646

Services
City Concierge — C-3
205 S. Shelby St. • 502-456-4478
Commonwealth Motorcycles — C-4
605 E. Jefferson St. • 502-589-2995
CrossFit The Ville — B-4
609 E. Market St. • 502-235-4546
Market Street Barbers — B-4
746 E. Market St. • 502-585-0002
Shine: a wellness studio — C-2
732 E. Jefferson St. • 502-442-2542

NuLu
East Market and East Main Streets
 corridor
Louisville, KY
www.nulu.com

Perhaps the most unique eatery in the district is the **Mayan Café**. Chef Bruce Ucan is a native of Mexico's Yucatan Peninsula and he has brought the savory flavors of that region with him to Louisville. *Cochinita pibil* is succulent, slow roasted pork served with seasoned, pan-roasted *tok-sel* lima beans. Creative cocktails are made with freshly squeezed juices, also refreshing on their own. Enjoy a drink with *sikel-pak*, a savory pumpkin seed dip made with roasted tomatoes and cilantro. (www.themayancafe.com)

Decca features a Euro-inspired menu and several levels of dining in a restored 19th century house. From a cellar lounge with live music, to a warren of dining rooms, and a second story deck overlooking a courtyard with fire pit, it offers a sophisticated experience. Dishes include duck liver terrine, linguini with Brussels sprouts and preserved lemon, and wood-grilled pork chop with polenta and mint. (www.deccarestaurant.com)

Located at the easternmost end of NuLu is **RYE** (www.ryeonmarket.com), also housed in a reclaimed historic house. Assemble dinner from a selection of small plates, such as green curry soup, chicken & egg toast, and pastrami-spiced beets. Or tuck into mains such as milk-braised pork shoulder or carrot agnolotti.

A great introduction to NuLu can be had on the first Friday evening of each month during the Trolley Hop from 5 to 11 p.m. Park your car in the lot at Louisville Slugger Field and take the free trolleys around the district to explore the shops, galleries, and eateries.

OLD 502 WINERY / FALLS CITY BREWERY
Urban Winery & Craft Brewery
LOUISVILLE

*I*t's a Friday evening at the end of the work week, and the tasting room at Old 502 Winery and Falls City Brewing is jammed. A mostly – but not exclusively – Millennial crowd surrounds the bar and occupies all the tables. Generous samples, for a modest fee, are being poured of both Old 502's wines and Falls City's brews. Patrons of the tasting room can see the gleaming fermentation tanks through a glass wall and shop for beer and wine accessories in the gift store.

Old 502 (That's Louisville's area code, by the way.) purports to be the only urban winery in Kentucky. No, there isn't a rooftop arbor or a grape-growing greenhouse tucked beneath the nearby interstate exit ramp. Winemaker Logan Leet sources his grapes "from about a dozen local vineyards when we can" and gets grapes from other states as well for the varied selection of wines he blends. These range from the sweet red Bach's Wine ("Music to Your Lips," a blend of Chambourcin and Concord) to the dry Bore-Dough ("Spelled Accordingly," Cabernet Franc, Malbec, Cabernet Sauvignon, Merlot).

The names reflect some of what Leet says helps set Old 502 apart from other Kentucky wineries. "Our differences lie in our marketing and labeling (maybe a little quirky), our Tasting Room/Gift Shop/Event Center (Downtown attitude and proud of it!), our proprietary blends (helps us retain consistency and uniqueness), and our winemaking process (we actually do some of our early processing on the site of other wineries in the region, helping those wineries and helping us grow faster without expanding our production space)."

Did he say "quirky?" Certainly the description on the label of B*%#@!N (Bourbon) Barrel Red (Chambourcin, Cabernet Sauvignon, Merlot), which Leet says is Old 502's most popular bottling, testifies to that, as well as to the winery's urban edginess:

> "Get past the busted sidewalks, boarded up buildings and the perpetual hum of 18-wheelers chugging across the overpass and you'll agree: the Western edge of downtown Louisville is an ideal location for winemaking. Aged 30 days in Kentucky oak barrels, Old 502 Winery's "B*%#@!N Barrel red" is all the proof you need."

And there's craft beer, too. In 2014, local brewery Falls City, with a name dating back to 1904, moved its brewing operations to the same building on 10th Street housing the winery. The current flagship iteration of the beer is an Extra Special English Pale Ale,

**Old 502 Winery /
Falls City Brewery**
120 S. Tenth Street
Louisville, KY 40202
(502) 540-5650
www.old502.com

Tuesday - Thursday:
  12 p.m. - 6 p.m.
Friday - Saturday:
  12 p.m. - 8 p.m.

less aggressively hoppy than American Pale Ale, and a little lower in alcohol by volume, too. It's served in the tasting room and sold in half-gallon growlers to take home. Falls City is also pretty easy to find around town. Cans and bottles are sold in groceries and liquor retail stores and found on draft, as well as in bottles, at restaurants and bars throughout Louisville.

The tasting room is open year-round. And while wine-drinkers certainly have the option of switching to beer here during the summer, Old 502 has another option for combating the heat. Sweeter wines are used to make decidedly adults-only treats – icily refreshing wine slushies.

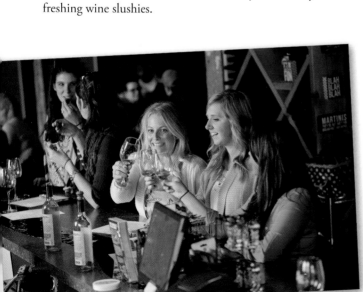

THE ORIGINAL BARDSTOWN ROAD FARMERS' MARKET

And Omelets, Too

LOUISVILLE

Louisville is large enough to support several farmers' markets, which are found in most areas of the city. And the market that started this Saturday morning shopping habit, the Bardstown Road Farmers' Market in the Highlands, organized in 1991, is still bringing area farmers and consumers together.

Squeezed into the parking lot of the Bardstown Road Presbyterian Church, the market is a bustling place, especially when the weather is fine. At the height of the harvest season, close to 30 growers bring their products, which include fresh-cut flowers, vegetables, fruits, and cheeses, as well as pasture-raised poultry, lamb, pork, beef, and bison. Baked goods, such as warm pastries, and bottled foods, such as preserves, jams, and honey, are also for sale.

It's not uncommon to have local musicians providing entertainment, adding to the festive atmosphere, which market manager Beth Nolte describes as, "A wonderful convergence of people looking for the best food in the world and the farmers selling it. It feels magical!"

The market can certainly be a place for discovery. Think bison is only used for steaks and, perhaps, burgers? Check out the Kentucky Bison booth where bison breakfast sausage, stew meat, baby back ribs, pot roast, and stir-fry cuts are also displayed. Looking for meat not often found in chain supermarkets, such

as fresh rabbit, quail, and goose? Valley Acre Farm sells it, along with free-range chickens, duck, and turkeys.

Patrons not only buy goods directly from the producers when they visit the market, they can sign up for a cheese of the month (from Boone Creek Creamery), register for a CSA (Community Supported Agriculture, i.e., food co-op), or enjoy breakfast from several of the vendors.

Tables and chairs are set up throughout the market. Highland Coffee is usually on hand, dispensing hot drinks (caffeinated and not) that can be enjoyed with Full Heart Farm's freshly baked breads (blueberry lemon, carrot cranberry coconut, banana walnut) and cookies (including oatmeal with pistachios and assorted seeds).

The Original Bardstown Road Farmers' Market
1722 Bardstown Road
Louisville, KY 40205
(502) 634-2868
www.bardstownroadfarmers-market.com

April - December
Saturdays:
  8 a.m. - 12 p.m.

January - March
Saturdays:
  10 a.m. - 12 p.m.

Dream Catcher Farm, which specializes in grass-fed meats, offers a hot breakfast menu that includes quiches, soups, biscuits and sausage gravy, cheese grits, and whole wheat bread and rolls.

But the signature breakfast at the Bardstown Road Farmers' Market has to be Ivor Chodkowski's omelets. Chodkowski is the proprietor of Field Day Family Farm, part-owner of Harvest (see p. 74), and one of the founders of the market.

The ingredients change based on what Chodkowski is harvesting and what culinary inspiration hits him. The eggs may wrap smoked catfish one Saturday and artisan cheese on another.

"He recently served an omelet with mild radishes sprinkled with coriander," said Nolte. "What a burst of flavor!"

Lemony Carrot 'Fettuccini' with Toasted Walnuts

This comes from one of Louisville food writer Phyllis Fitzgerald's columns. She regularly writes for the Bardstown Road Farmers' Market. It takes advantage of the fall produce.

½ c. chopped walnuts
2 lbs. large carrots, peeled, stem ends discarded
1 ¼ c. low-sodium chicken or vegetable broth, divided
1 T. grated lemon zest
Salt and ground black pepper
2 oz. Neufchatel (low-fat cream cheese)
1 t. lemon juice
2 T. chopped fresh chives

• Heat the oven to 350 degrees F.
• In a shallow baking dish, spread the walnuts in an even layer and bake on the oven's middle shelf for 8 to 10 minutes, or until they smell fragrant. Remove and set aside.
• Meanwhile, using a swivel blade or a Y-shaped vegetable peeler, peel the carrots into long fettuccine-like strands, discarding the core (or saving it for a snack or a stock).
• In a large skillet, combine 1 cup of the chicken broth with the lemon zest, a hefty pinch of salt and several grinds of pepper. Whisk the mixture until the lemon is well distributed.
• Cut up the cheese into small pieces and add it to the skillet along with the carrots. Cover the skillet tightly and bring the broth to a boil. Reduce the heat and simmer the carrots, covered, for 3 minutes. Remove the lid, and stir the carrots gently with tongs to make sure the cheese is well distributed. Cover and simmer, adding the additional broth if the mixture seems dry, for another 1 to 2 minutes, or just until the carrots are tender. Stir in the lemon juice, then season with salt and pepper. Divide the carrot "fettuccine" between 4 serving plates, then top each portion with a quarter of the toasted walnuts and the chives.

Serves 4.

PAUL'S FRUIT MARKETS
Source of Kentucky Specialty Foodstuffs
LOUISVILLE

*P*aul's Fruit Market traces its origin to founder Paul Thieneman's 1940s open-air, seasonal produce store. During the 1950s he built his business, and competed with the rising national supermarket chains, by introducing then-exotic citrus from Florida and California to the Louisville area, and selling beautiful fruit-based gift baskets.

The four Paul's locations today are enclosed, open year-round, and owned and managed by a third generation of the family – siblings Phil and Sally Thieneman and Mary Hartman. The shops still attract patrons with their colorful outdoor seasonal stock of herbs and flower flats in the spring, hanging baskets in summer, pumpkins and gourds in fall, and evergreens in winter.

So, do not be misled by the name. Paul's has grown well beyond fruit. It is a one-stop store for a whole range of local specialty foods.

This variety includes very local products, such as Benedictine spread and Henry Bain's sauce, as well as Kentucky Proud™ fruit, vegetables, meats, sauces, candies, and baked goods. Among these are many of the flours and grits from Weisenberger Mills (p. 34), sauces from Moonlite Bar-B-Q (p. 170), Kenny's Farmhouse Cheeses (p. 156), and a range of spices and sauces from Bourbon Barrel Foods (p. 58). The stores recently added butch-

er shops, which cook locally purchased country ham and sell it sliced to order.

The butchers arrived from Burger's Supermarket, another third-generation neighborhood grocery that closed in 2013 when the owners retired. Along with the meat men, came Bethany, the beaten biscuit maker. The traditional Southern recipe specifies beating the dough until it blisters, a very labor-intensive operation. So, special machines, resembling wooden wringers, were invented for processing the dough. To the uninitiated, these small round biscuits, with the crimped sides and tops marked with fork holes, are a mystery. They're hard. They crumble when cut. They seem inedible.

But pop them in a hot oven for a few minutes and they pull apart into two perfect, densely layered halves ready to receive tender slices of salty country ham, ideally dressed with a smidgen of Durkee's sauce.

Paul's Fruit Markets
12119 Shelbyville Road
Louisville, KY 40243
(502) 253-0072
www.paulsfruit.com

Other Locations
3922 Chenoweth Square
Louisville, KY 40207
(502) 896-8918

4946 Brownsboro Road
Louisville, KY 40222
(502) 426-5070

3704 Taylorsville Road
Louisville, KY 40220
(502) 456-4750

Monday - Saturday:
 8 a.m. - 7 p.m.
Sunday:
 10 a.m. - 6 p.m.

The in-house deli makes a variety of spreads, including standbys such as pimento cheese ham, and egg and chicken salads. The native Louisville spread is Benedictine, a pale green cream cheese, cucumber, and onion preparation traditionally served on very thin slices of white bread. Louisville caterer Jennie Benedict created it in the early part of the 20th century. Many Louisville restaurants serve a BBLT – Benedictine, bacon, lettuce and tomato sandwich.

Beaten Biscuits

Another eponymous Louisville food found at Paul's is Henry Bain's Sauce, invented more than a century ago by head waiter Henry Bain at the city's private Pendennis Club as a condiment for meat. Excellent on pork or beef tenderloin, think of it as Worcestershire on steroids, since its savory flavor is pumped up with the addition of pickled walnuts and anchovies.

Among sweets, Paul's carries Bauer's Modjeskas (see p. 14), many brands of bourbon balls, and the only fruitcake that may not be the subject of jokes. Gethsemani Fruit Cake is handmade by the Trappist monks of the Abbey of Gethsemani near Bardstown. Nutty, spicy, and very, very moist, the key ingredient is a generous lashing of that favorite Kentucky ingredient – bourbon. Look for the Gethsemani bourbon chocolate fudge, too.

SHUCKMAN'S FISH CO. & SMOKERY
Bourbon Barrel Smoked Fish, Spoonfish Caviar
LOUISVILLE

The American Paddlefish, *Polyodon spathula*, is known as the Spoonfish in culinary circles. It lives near the muddy bottoms of the Ohio, Missouri, and Mississippi Rivers where adults grow to an average of five to six feet long, weigh 60 pounds or more, and are easily recognized by the long, flat, paddle-like projection from their heads. At first sighting, the shark-like Spoonfish does not seem a likely candidate for the table. But the Spoonfish is related to the sturgeon, and thus is the source of excellent American caviar.

Lewis Shuckman processes and sells Spoonfish caviar at his business, founded by his grandfather in 1919, in West Louisville, just a few minutes' drive from the fish's Ohio River habitat. (His source for both roe and fish filets, which he smokes, is a Kentucky fish farm.) He operates Shuckman's Fish Co. in partnership with his wife Vicki and their daughter Lauren.

The Shuckmans seem to have come straight from Hollywood Central Casting as the Family of Jovial Fishmongers. "Fun" is one of Lewis's favorite words. (He is obviously delighted to be smoking and selling seafood.) Vicki's grandchildren call her "Mimi" and that's the name on the company's line of spreads, including beer cheese and Benedictine. Lauren beams with pride as she discusses the fine points of the firm's caviar, which has been praised (and served) by renowned chefs Rick Bayless of Chicago and Atlanta's Ford Fry.

In addition to processing the famed caviar, Shuckman's also smokes Kentucky trout and Norwegian and Scottish salmon. The latter is used in a variety of products, from alder smoked salmon slices (a 10-hour process very similar to that used by Native Americans) to Italian-style salmon sausages, lean and savory salmon burgers, and a creamy smoked salmon spread.

Hickory wood and applewood are also employed for smoking. And not surprisingly, since this is a Kentucky fish smokery, bourbon barrel char is used, too. But not just any bourbon barrels.

"We get our barrels from the Van Winkles," says Lewis Shuckman, with a distinct twinkle in his eye. The rare and expensive Old Rip Van Winkle and

Shuckman's Fish Co. & Smokery
3001 W. Main Street
Louisville, KY 40212
(502) 775-6478
www.kysmokedfish.com

Monday - Friday:
8 a.m. - 3 p.m.

Pappy Van Winkle bourbons have a cult following and he gestures to a couple of the prized, but now empty, barrels sitting in a corner of the pristinely clean smokehouse. Since the bourbons age so long in their barrels (a decade and more), there's a lot of whiskey soaked into the wood that imparts rich bourbony flavor to his fish.

Many of the Shuckmans' products are sold in area groceries. Visitors are always welcome to stop by the shop located in the front of the processing operation. But probably the most convenient way to buy their products is through the company's website where each is described in delectable detail. Other offerings include smoked whitefish spread, crab spread, and shrimp spread. There is also an archive of recipes with serving suggestions.

Since it's very hard to choose, know that a Sampler is available, which includes two ounces of caviar, smoked Nova Salmon, Smoked Kentucky Rainbow Trout, Smoked Alder Salmon, Salmon Burgers, and Smoked Salmon Spread.

That's a party in a box!

Benedictine

Stuffed Eggs with Spoonfish Caviar

12 hard-boiled eggs
1 small roasted red pepper, chopped fine
½ c. ricotta cheese
¼ c. sour cream
¼ t. salt
Pepper to taste
1 ½ T. fresh chives, chopped fine
Fresh chives for garnish
Spoonfish caviar

• Shell the eggs; cut in half lengthwise and remove the yolks.
• Sieve the egg yolks and ricotta cheese into a bowl. Add the sour cream, roasted red pepper, chopped chives, salt, and pepper to taste.
• With a pastry bag and large star clip, pipe the mixture into the hollows of the egg whites. Garnish with fresh chives and top with Spoonfish Caviar as desired.

83

GALLREIN FARMS
Produce + Petting Zoo
SHELBYVILLE

*B*ill and Randie Gallrein aren't just farming. They are educating. With every aspect of their operation – greenhouse flowers and produce, acres of sweet corn, the rolling pumpkin patch, and a farmyard full of friendly animals comprising the petting zoo – the Gallreins have made opportunities for the city-dwelling public to see what a working farm is about.

There's so much to do that visitors will be rewarded by multiple visits.

Gardeners will want to visit as soon as the farm opens in the spring, when the nine greenhouses are filled with a huge selection of bedding flowers and vegetables. There's a bakery/café open for lunch Monday through Saturday from 11 a.m. to 2 p.m., so time a visit to take advantage of the opportunity to sample farm-fresh fare. Toward the end of May is when strawberries come in season. They are available in the farm store, or visitors can pick them themselves.

Summer is when the beans, squash, apples, tomatoes, okra, and other fresh fruits and vegetables are harvested. It's also the beginning of the season for what is probably the Gallreins' signature crop, sweet corn, sold by the pound and by the bushel in the farm store.

Green Gallrein logo tee-shirts and caps worn by the farm staff match the paint on the John Deere tractors and combines they operate, harvesting and packing corn daily through the harvest season. The whirr of

machinery provides the backdrop of farm sounds supplemented by the high-pitched voices of children discovering the feathered and furred fun of the petting zoo.

Children and adults are invited to feed the chickens and pigs and pet the donkeys and goats. There

Gallrein Farms
1029 Vigo Road
Shelbyville, KY 40065
(502) 633-4849
www.gallreinfarms.com

April - September
 Monday - Saturday:
  9 a.m. - 6 p.m.
 Sunday:
  1 p.m. - 5 p.m.

October
 Saturday:
  10 a.m. - 6 p.m.
 Sunday:
  1 p.m. - 5 p.m.

are some decidedly not-your-expected farm animals, too. Levi the Camel, for example, puts paid to the stereotype of the cantankerous "ship of the desert." No spitting or biting on his part. Just patient, furry charm.

The growing season may be winding down, but a fall visit is just as busy as any other time. Take a stroll in the pumpkin patch to pick out the perfect potential jack o' lantern. Or spend an adventurous hour or so trying to solve the puzzle of the corn maze. Perhaps the perfect ending to a year of visiting the farm is to take a hayride around the property before stocking up on produce in the farm store.

85

MULBERRY ORCHARD
Peaches, Apples, and Some Special Bees
SHELBYVILLE

$\mathcal{P}$each lovers will want to make a beeline for Mulberry Orchard when it opens to visitors in late June because it would be hard to find any fresher fruit. Farmers Amanda and Matt Gajdjik (She's a sixth generation Shelby County farmer. He's a newbie.) leave their peaches ripening on the trees, soaking up sun and accumulating sugar, up until the peak moment for picking. What Amanda Gajdjik describes as "the most sweet and juicy" peaches you'll encounter are then taken straight from the orchard at the back of the farm to the farm store.

With hayrides, a playground, and a lunch menu and picnic tables, Mulberry Orchard easily qualifies as a great place for a family to spend a morning or afternoon. In late summer and fall, 15 varieties of peaches are replaced by 15 varieties of apples, which are also carefully monitored and picked at just the right moment.

"We see the same faces every year coming for the peaches, and then it changes to the customers coming for apples," observed Gajdjik. She finds it interesting that the peach people and the apple people have virtually no overlap. Perhaps the phrase should be "compare apples to peaches" instead of "compare apples to oranges."

While the farm's name is "Mulberry Orchard," the trees are a relatively recent addition. They joined traditional Kentucky row crops – soybeans, corn, and tobacco. The family raises beef cattle, too, so the processed meat from their herd is featured in the hamburgers served here. Neighboring farms contribute close to 100 varieties of vegetables, as well as other farm-fresh meats.

The fall menu will feature a pulled pork sandwich which is served on a pretzel bun and garnished with apple slices as are the deli sandwiches. The sweet cole slaw contains apples, too. Depending on the season, hand-sized fried peach and/or apple pies are offered as well.

The farm store also sells honey made by bees that pollinate the orchard's trees. It happens that Amanda Gajdjik's mother, Pat Hornback, not only has the farm next door, she is also the president of the Shelby

Mulberry Orchard
1330 Mulberry Pike
Shelbyville, KY 40065
(502) 655-2633
www.mulberryorchardky.com

Late June - October
  Wednesday - Saturday:
    9 a.m. - 6 p.m.
  Sunday:
    1 p.m. - 5 p.m.

County Beekeepers' Association and has hives both on her property and on her daughter and son-in-law's.

Hornback is passionate about teaching other people about beekeeping and honey. She offers instruction through the beekeepers' association (Anyone can join for just $5.) and about once a year holds her class at Mulberry Orchard.

"I don't use any chemicals in my hives," she explains. "Most beekeepers choose to use approved chemical insecticide strips inside hives. These chemicals can stay in the wax comb for several years. I choose not to take the easy route. More hive management, problems with mites, but my bees have to be strong and I will not use chemicals. I do all the work myself, offer "newbies" out to the farm to join in the fun. You can see my hives and come jar your own. Doesn't get more transparent than that!" To find out about beekeeping and honey classes, e-mail her at pmh@shelbybb.net.

Pork sanwich on a Pretzel bun

87

SWALLOW RAIL FARM
Pasture-Raised Poultry and Lamb
SIMPSONVILLE

*J*eneen Wiche recalls how her 20-acre farm got its name, "Daddy named it that because before so many little subdivisions popped up around us, there were lots of farms and barns. The barn swallow population was pretty significant. Two railroad tracks flanked Conner Station at the end of our road. So Swallow Rail."

"Daddy" was Wiche's late father, journalist and gardening expert Fred Wiche, a well-known and respected Louisville media figure for decades. Jeneen Wiche and her husband, Andy Smart, now raise pasture-fed chickens and lamb on the farm. And their barn, which had primarily been used for storage in her father's time, is now used in the livestock operation and boasts a thriving population of swallows itself.

The chickens Wiche and Smart tend are Freedom Rangers, a breed developed in France in the 1960s. "They take longer to mature than typical broilers," explains Wiche. "About 10 weeks to get to full size, about four and a half pounds."

With handsome red, grey, and bronze plumage, the Freedom Rangers are also "more athletic" says Wiche, since they are out and about in the pastures. This gives their meat a firm texture.

These are larger, leaner birds than typically found in supermarkets. Since they are more evenly proportioned (most chickens are raised to have a high proportion of breast meat),

most of the meat tends toward the richer flavor and texture associated with the darker legs and thighs.

The 10-week cycle of raising and pasturing chicks and chickens may sound complicated, but Wiche say

Swallow Rail Farm
2340 Conner Station Road
Simpsonville, KY 40067
(502) 722-2997
www.swallowrailfarm.com

No regular hours, but customers are welcome to call and pick up orders anytime.

what she is doing is relatively simple. "If someone wants to buy chicken or lamb, all they have to do is call and arrange a time to come by. Then we look in the freezer and pick out what they want."

Typically, the farm will have about 45 sheep on its pastures, too, usually processed four at a time and sold as whole or half animals, butchered into several cuts.

The Swallow Rail chickens also lay eggs, which are sold year-round via a CSA. Customers can order one to three dozen eggs, which are distributed every two weeks to a handful of Louisville locations. They can also be collected from the farm.

Harvest Coffee & Café in Shelbyville (524 Main Street, (502) 633-8090) has a mostly vegetarian menu, but the café buys chickens from Swallow Rail. "Chef Bill makes an awesome chicken salad with the meat," says Wiche. "He makes incredible stock from the chicken, too."

Wiche notes that her customers are happy to pay for premium products. The value is in quality over quantity. "Meat shouldn't be cheap and we shouldn't eat so much of it."

How to Prepare Freedom Ranger Chicken

Jeneen Wiche offers this advice for cooking leaner, pasture raised chicken:

"My experience cooking the Freedom Rangers is a bit different than cooking conventional roasters raised indoors. The Freedom Ranger raised on pasture has more Omega 3 and less saturated fat and has not been injected with anything. Plus the ratio of meat in the legs, thighs, and breast is more proportional. If you ask any of our regular customers, they say the stand out difference is in the 'texture of the meat and a richer flavor'. So, to get a juicy bird, we recommend cooking them at a higher heat and shorter time than people are used to. For a whole bird (our ideal is 4.5 lbs.), I will preheat the convection oven to 450 degrees F. and cook for 30 minutes; turn it down to 400 degrees F. for another 30 minutes. If the bird is smaller, I will cut back about 5 minutes. Let it rest for a few minutes before carving – it really does hold the juice in!"

For a ½ chicken (at about 2.25 lbs.), cook 15 minutes at 450 degrees F. and another 30 minutes at 400 degrees F.

Grass fed meat has a reputation for cooking in about 30% less time.

AMBROSIA FARMS
Heirloom Tomatoes
FINCHVILLE

Old German, White Wonder, Black from Tula, Kentucky Beefsteak, Solar Flare, Emerald Apple, Orange Oxheart, White Beauty, Peppermint, and Black Mammoth. In Kentucky this might be a list of horses entered in a race on any given day at Churchill Downs. But in fact, it is a very small sampling of the more than 80 varieties of heirloom tomatoes Brooke Eckmann cultivates on her Ambrosia Farm in Shelby County.

A former teacher, Eckmann only started farming fulltime in 2011, but she and her tomatoes have quickly become favorites with some of nearby Louisville's most acclaimed chefs.

Anthony Lamas is the chef/owner at Seviche (www.sevicherestaurant.com), an award-winning Latin American restaurant that specializes in sustainable menu items, from produce to seafood. "Brooke is amazing," says Lamas. "She is so passionate about what she is doing. People like to call chefs rock stars, but she *is* the rock star!"

Lamas discovered Eckmann and her produce at a Louisville farmers' market. He introduced her to other area chefs, but their collaboration has become especially strong. While she provides produce for several restaurants' seasonal multi-course tomato dinners, Lamas takes his restaurant to her farm.

In the elegantly restored former tobacco barn where she lays out tomato tastings for chefs so they can place orders with her, Eckmann and Lamas set up the tables for the annual Farmer & Chef Barn Dinner in September. One year, courses included an Heirloom Tomato Celebration (with Japanese basil garlic pesto, lemon aioli, grilled bread), Shrimp a la Parilla (radish, blistered shishitos, cucumber slaw, roasted heirloom salsa), and Wood-Grilled Pork Loin (poblano Manchego grits, heirloom tomato bourbon BBQ, country ham demi-glace).

Lamas also explains that Eckmann has "set aside 10 acres for me" in which she grows chili peppers, radishes, peanuts, and other produce he uses at Seviche.

Ambrosia Farms
5123 Buck Creek Road
Finchville, KY 40022
(502) 457-0033
www.facebook.com/AmbrosiaFarm

Seasonal Wednesday evening tomato tastings in the farm store. Call for seasonal hours or check the Facebook page.

"Because of demand, I have several acres of non-GMO corn," explains Eckmann, who gestures in the direction of the field with hands lined with soil, apparently permanently imbedded from digging her crops. (Her hands are the only aspect of Ambrosia Farm that isn't spotless or meticulously ordered.)

She holds up a large jar of pale red liquid which she identifies as "tomato water." Quite different from tomato juice, the water is made by straining tomatoes through cheesecloth. "Add a little bourbon to it. It's delicious!" she promises.

Eckmann is delighted to guide visitors through weekly tastings when her tomatoes are in season, from early August to late September. "The White Wonder has a high sugar content. It's very mild and sweet. This Russian heirloom (Black from Tula) is interestingly spicy."

The variety is truly impressive. Orange Oxheart is so sweet that it tastes like candy. The Snowball is faintly lemony. Black Mammoth, a tomato with purple-brown flesh developed in Kazakhstan, has so many layers of savory, fruity flavors that it is almost like a fine wine.

With a little planning and weekly summer visits, it's possible to taste all 80 plus varieties of Eckmann's heirlooms, at least for now.

"I'm always looking for new ones. I may be growing more than 100 different kinds soon."

Heirloom Tomato Gazpacho
From Chef Anthony Lamas at Seviche. Serve cold.

1 red bell pepper, seeds removed
1 yellow bell pepper, seeds removed
1 poblano pepper, seeds removed
4 heirloom tomatoes (Whichever you fancy.)
4 cucumbers, peeled and seeds removed
Juice of 2 limes
Juice of 2 lemons
¼ c. chopped Spanish onion
2 cloves fresh garlic
½ c. olive oil
1 jalapeno
2 c. ice water
1 T. kosher salt
1 T. white pepper

• Puree all ingredients together in a blender.
• Refrigerate for at least 2 hours.

Serves 4 as an appetizer.

LIMESTONE BRANCH DISTILLERY
Craft Moonshine Distillers
LEBANON

When visitors ask someone in Kentucky how to become a bourbon distiller, the frequent answer is "It helps if your name happens to be Beam." It's said tongue-in-cheek, but the humor contains a large measure of truth.

Jacob Beam started distilling spirits in central Kentucky around 1795, decades before corn-based whiskey came to be called "bourbon." His descendants (including Jim Beam, whose name is attached to the largest-selling bourbon in the world) made bourbon for four more generations before Prohibition interfered. Other descendants included M. C. Beam, who produced T. J. Pottinger and Old Trump bourbons in the early 1900s, and his son, Guy Beam, who was a master distiller for many companies, including Old Trump and Yellowstone, before Prohibition sent him to Canada to ply his trade.

After Repeal, Beams started distilling again, some for Jim Beam (now an international corporation) and others for Heaven Hill (the second largest privately-held spirits company in the United States.)

In 2012, Guy Beam's grandsons, brothers Steve and Paul Beam (descended on their mother's side from another legendary distillery, J. W. Dant), opened their own craft distillery in Marion County, not far from Jacob's original operation. The minimalist exterior of the stone and metal building housing Limestone Branch Distillery gives no hint of the generations of history found within.

Just inside the entrance, the Beam brothers (a seventh generation of distilling Beams) have dedicated space to a combination gift shop and mini-museum of their bourbon-making history. Visitors see glass-front-

ed cases filled with distilling memorabilia, including vintage advertisements and bourbon bottles. A guide uses many of these artifacts to describe the family's history before the tour passes through doors into the distillery itself.

It's not uncommon to find Steve Beam in the compact distillery watching over the custom-made copper pot still from Hoga of Spain. The small still only produces enough distillate at a time to fill a single barrel. At present, most of what is being made is actually not bourbon, which would need to age in barrels for several years before achieving the Beams' desired quality. The Beam brothers are proudly making high quality, quite legal, moonshine.

Beam explains, "What we are making is sugar shine. It's distilled from 50 percent fermented corn and 50 percent fermented cane sugar. And we use white corn from Weisenberger Mills."

It's a common misconception that "moonshine" is synonymous with "raw whiskey." The latter is the clear

Limestone Branch Distillery
1280 Veterans Memorial Highway
Lebanon, KY 40033
(270) 699-9004
www.limestonebranch.com

Monday - Saturday:
  10 a.m. - 5 p.m.
Sunday:
  1 p.m. - 5 p.m.

Tours begin on the hour.

spirit distilled from corn-predominant sour mash that becomes "bourbon" when it goes into oak containers.

"Authentic moonshine from this area of Kentucky contains sugar," says Beam, who walks visitors though the process of cooking, fermentation, distilling, and bottling, all of which take place in the same room.

The tour ends in the tasting room where jug-shaped glass bottles of 'shine are lined up on the handsome wood bar. The strongest product is T. J. Pottinger Sugar Shine (100 proof), which is certainly sweet, but not cloying. Infused moonshines, weighing in between 40 and 50 proofs, include jalapeno, cherry, strawberry, blackberry, and apple-cinnamon pie. "We infuse the spirits with natural flavors after distillation," Beam notes.

Limestone Branch also has an agreement with the bakers of the famous MoonPie pastries, to make another line of flavored shine. Billed as "MoonPie with a kick," MoonPie Moonshine is available in vanilla, chocolate, and banana flavors.

The Beams are making a couple of aged products, too. Precinct No. 6 employs the same stone-ground white corn from Weisenberger Mills used in their moonshine, as well as fermented cane sugar. The distillate is then aged in barrels previously used for aging bourbon and bottled at 95.6 proof. This "sugar whiskey" has a distinctive sweet corn character.

And naturally, given their heritage, they are making bourbon. The first batch was distilled and barreled shortly after Limestone Branch started operating. It should be mature enough to bottle in 2015. Plus, the company has partnered with Luxco of St. Louis, the company that bought the Yellowstone brand name years ago, to start producing Yellowstone in Kentucky again.

"We should also have selected barrels from Yellowstone's existing stock [in summer 2015]," reports Beam.

Chocolate Milkshake
Very much a milkshake for grown-ups!

3 scoops Chocolate Ice Cream
½ c. of milk
2 shots Chocolate MoonPie Moonshine
Chocolate syrup (to taste)
Marshmallow Fluff, graham cracker crumbs, whipped cream, and a cherry (garnish)

• Combine first four ingredients in a blender and blend until smooth.
• Dip the rim of a Mason jar in marshmallow fluff and roll in graham cracker crumbs.
• Pour milkshake in the Mason jar and garnish with whipped cream, chocolate syrup, and a cherry.
Substitute Vanilla Ice Cream and Vanilla MoonPie Moonshine for Vanilla Milkshake.

*O*nly about a half hour's drive east of Limestone Branch Distillery, Penn's Store seems far more remote. The roads narrow from four lanes to two. Asphalt gives way to gravel. The car trip is relatively short, but it represents a journey much farther back in time.

Penn's little wooden building seems to sag against the foot of the forested hillside where a general store has been located since before the Civil War. In fact, this is the oldest country store in the United States still owned and operated by the same family. Penns have owned it since 1850. Jeanne Penn Lane, the fifth generation since the first Penn owner, is the manager/owner now. Her daughter, Dawn Osborn, frequently works behind the counter.

On this slightly chilly Saturday morning in September, a memory of mist from the nearby North Rolling Fork River and Little South Creek hangs in the air. Penn's prides itself on being a "meeting place" and the locals are indeed meeting and greeting. Old men in tractor caps park vintage pick-up trucks near the front of the store. Dogs and children wander around the lawn in front of banks yellow with autumn asters, and the trees are beginning to show a touch of fall color. The sagging screen door creaks open and slaps back against its wooden frame when patrons enter the store.

Inside is an Aladdin's Cave of memorabilia and merchandise, most of which is for sale. Soap powder, dishwashing liquid, canned soups, tinned meats, bags of chips, boxes of crackers, candy bars, jars of hard candy, gum, cookies, soft drinks, wooden utensils, knick knacks, gourds, and bunches of dried herbs from the garden next to the store all vie for attention. A cast iron wood stove takes up a good deal of floor space, but it's not cold enough to press it into service. Along the wall, near the ceiling, are rows of photos of famous visitors, mostly country music artists such as Ricky Skaggs and Chet Atkins.

Penn's Store
257 Penn's Store Road
Gravel Switch, KY 40328
(859) 332-7715
www.pennsstore.com

April - November
 Saturday:
  11 a.m. - 5 p.m.
 Sunday:
  2 p.m. - 5 p.m.

November - April
 Saturday:
  11 a.m. - 4 p.m.
 Sunday:
  2 p.m. - 4 p.m.

Penn's Store is listed on the National Register of Historic Places and is designated a Kentucky Historical Landmark. But there are many good reasons to visit other than to shop in the manner of your great-grandparents or to marvel that the ramshackle building is actually still standing.

The second Sunday of every month "Picking and Singing Live" takes place at the store. Everyone is invited to bring an instrument and a chair and join in the jam sessions. (To get a preview of this, go to PennsStoreKy on YouTube.) GPS (Gossip/Poetry/Story Telling) Sessions are held on the third Sunday of every month. Anyone is welcome to contribute, or simply listen to the discussion. There are three seasonal events, too.

During the last weekend in April, the store hosts the Kentucky Writers Day Celebration and Songwriters Showcase, where visitors can take in performances, buy books and recordings, and even buy bedding plants for their summer gardens.

In 1992, the first restroom facility, Penn's Privy, was installed at the store. That occasion is commemorated yearly with the "Great Outhouse Blowout" on the first Saturday after Labor Day. Teams with whimsically designed outhouses on wheels race around a 300-foot course. The race is a small part of a day-long arts and crafts and food fair.

"Bounty of the Season" takes place the Friday and Saturday of Thanksgiving weekend. Look for handmade ornaments, gifts, cards, and other Christmas items.

Call the store, or check out the website, to confirm all events.

HINTON'S ORCHARD & FARM MARKET
New Uses for Old Farm Buildings
HODGENVILLE

*J*eremy Hinton readily admits to being a thief. "I don't hesitate to steal a good idea when I see one," he acknowledged with a grin on a bright summer morning while waiting for a school group to visit his farm. Hinton, who operates his family's business with his wife Joanna and their children Jacob, Joslyn, and Joel, was referring to the way he has creatively repurposed several farm elements.

For example, when visiting another farm he saw a play area had been set up using corn in place of sand in a sandbox. He had the perfect, and very appropriate, place to do the same. Two big metal grain bins sporting conical roofs were no longer being used to store grain. Rather than tear them down, Hinton turned them into playrooms, with boxes filled with corn. Visiting children are fascinated. And no one goes home with sand in her or his shoes. The other bin features a play market and kitchen, where young visitors can select toy produce and learn how to cook it.

Playground equipment, including slides and swings, are set up near the grain bins, as well as picnic tables where visitors can enjoy lunch. A decommissioned tractor is equipped with steps so little people (or grown-ups for

that matter) can climb on, and pretend to drive it themselves.

Lots of farms offer hayrides. But at the Hintons', instead of a flatbed trailer stacked with hay bales, a tractor pulls a large cotton wagon lined with bales. This vehicle has high, cage-like walls that riders can see through, but that guarantee no one will accidentally tumble off if the wagon hits a bump in a field.

The farm's dogs like to jump up for a ride when Hinton drives a school group on a meandering trip through the orchard containing nearly 2000 apple, peach, and pear trees and past the berry patches and green houses before returning to the front of the farm store building.

Joanna Hinton spends a lot of her time overseeing the store, which is well-stocked with whatever fruits and vegetables are in season on the farm. In spring there's asparagus, then the berry season (blueberries, strawberries, blackberries) arrives. By midsummer,

**Hinton's Orchard &
Farm Market**
8631 Campbellsville Road
Hodgenville, KY 42748
(270) 325-3854
www.hintonorchard.com

the peaches are being harvested, then apples and pears. Throughout the year there is an impressive array of preserves, jams, jellies, salsas, salad dressings, pickles, honey, fruit and vegetable butters (apple, pear, pumpkin), and bottles of fruit ciders. Freezer cases are stocked with meats from nearby farms specializing in beef, poultry, and pork.

Fall is the time for both selecting a pumpkin from one of the patches covering eight acres (and containing almost 60 pumpkin varieties) and for wandering through the three-acre corn maze. The maze features about a mile of trails and a scavenger hunt. Those looking for a special challenge can visit during the select Flashlight Corn Maze nights in October.

Obviously, Hinton's can be a busy place, especially on weekends or when a school group is visiting. But it's also possible to enjoy a quiet respite on the front porch of the farm store where chairs overlooking the grounds are arrayed for visitors' comfort. Enjoy an ice cream cone, watch birds flying over the orchard, and listen to the hum of insects.

97

STULL'S COUNTRY STORE
"If We Don't Have It, You Don't Need It"
PAYNEVILLE

*E*xamination of the map of the Ohio River as it meanders along the northern boundary of Kentucky reveals an odd lump of land with a couple of finger-like peninsulas jutting into the river west of Louisville. This is Meade County, home to both Fort Knox and thousands of acres of flat, rich farmland. Two-lane state highways here are bounded on both sides by miles of corn and soybean fields with an occasional farmhouse or barn rising from the ocean of crops.

Along one of these highways (KY 144), perched at the edge of the blacktop and surrounded on three sides by a wide cornfield, is a plain white building mostly noticeable for a clutch of gas pumps out front. This is Stull's Country Store, which has a brass plaque on its wooden front door that reads, "On this day in 1897 nothing happened." Well, even in its seeming rural isolation, plenty is happening at Stull's now.

Do not be fooled by the store's logo, which features a likeness of one of the rocking chairs on the front porch. This place is a whirlwind of activity. At lunchtime it's packed with locals who come for the liver cheese or smoked bologna sandwiches, not to mention the pulled pork barbecue, prepared daily in the iron smoker behind the store and served up by the sandwich and sold by the pound. (The barbecue sauce is homemade and sold by the bottle, too.)

The meat counter is presided over by butcher Mike Hartley, who explained to a visitor, "I was a junior in high school when I got off the bus in front of the store and started working. I never left." His very amicable boss is Marlinda (Maury) Stull, whose parents bought the store in 1972.

Stull loves her community and has never met a stranger. She explains that her store thrives in an era of chains and the Internet because, "Folks want something that harkens back to simpler times. They yearn for it. They know when they shop with us that we truly care. We care about them, their families, their neighbors and the community at large. We try to give them the best service, products, experience and freshest food we can. They know they are always welcomed, that we will go out of our way if we can to get what they need."

Stull's Country Store
4385 Rhodelia Road
Payneville, KY 40157
(270) 496-4169
www.stullscountrystore.com

Spring - Summer
 Monday - Friday:
  7 a.m. - 7 p.m.
 Saturday:
  8 a.m. - 7 p.m.
 Sunday:
  9 a.m. - 3 p.m.

Fall - Winter
 Monday - Friday:
  7 a.m. - 6:30 p.m.
 Saturday:
  8 a.m. - 7 p.m.
 Sunday:
  9 a.m. - 3 p.m.

The store has been in business since the turn of the nineteenth into the twentieth century. But that doesn't mean it's stocked with anachronisms. (Except, perhaps for an impressive selection of tobacco products.) In addition to the meat counter, there are aisles stocked with fresh produce, staples such as flour, cereal, canned goods, and spices. Coca Cola is sold as it should be, in six-ounce glass bottles. There's an unexpected, and excellent, selection of craft beers. (Maury Stull holds a beer tasting every spring.) And since it is a store very much catering to its farming community, there's livestock feed, seeds for flowers and vegetables, and a selection of tractor caps and tee-shirts sporting the Stull's logo. In other words, the place very much lives up to its motto, "If we don't have it, you don't need it!"

NORTHERN RIVER REGION

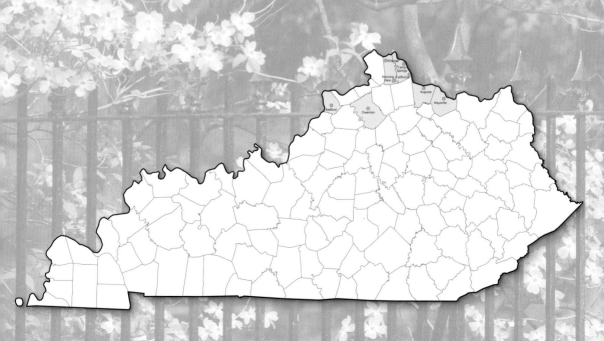

The hilly terrain of Northern Kentucky affords several beautiful Ohio River overlooks. Some feature the skyline of Cincinnati and others simply of a wide, winding ribbon of water dotted with coal-laden barges and other river traffic. One of the most scenic drives takes you along KY Highway 8 as it parallels the river between Augusta and Maysville. In places, the road is right at the water's edge.

There's something about this particular landscape that feels almost European and quite different from the rest of north central Kentucky. This may have something to do with the great number of German immigrants who settled in the Ohio Valley in the early to middle 19th century and found that the area reminded them of the Rhineland. They brought along their culinary culture and so many winemakers, brewers, and butchers started businesses in the Cincinnati and Northern Kentucky region.

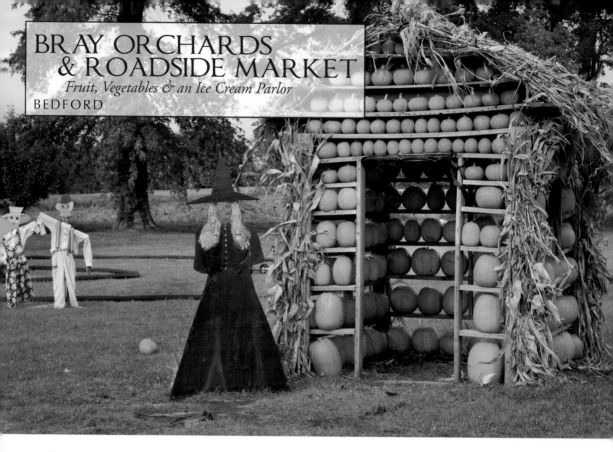

BRAY ORCHARDS & ROADSIDE MARKET
Fruit, Vegetables & an Ice Cream Parlor
BEDFORD

Traveling along I-71 at 70 mph and sharing multiple lanes with schools of hulking vehicles – 18-wheelers, vans, trailers, buses – it is hard to remember that the winding, two-lane U.S. Highway 42 roughly paralleling the interstate used to be the main route between Louisville and Cincinnati.

The roadside business at Bray Orchards grew along with America's pre-interstate highway system. Current owner Jamae Bray Pyles's family started selling apples and produce from a small stand in the 1930s, when customers traveling between the region's two largest cities arrived in Hudsons and Packards rather than Toyotas and SUV's. It might seem inevitable that Bray's business would have dwindled with the traffic after the interstate opened in the 1970s. But today the market has expanded and enjoys a local clientele who happily take I-71 Exit 28 (from Louisville) or Exit 44 (from Cincinnati) to shop here.

Driving north on U.S. 42, the market will be on left, with the orchard across the road to the right. The fields containing the vegetable gardens stretch out behind the market. A farm pond on the property has been a favorite of visitors for generations.

The front porch of the market building showcases Bray's seasonal offerings, from hanging flower baskets in spring, to multi-colored Indian corn and a dazzling variety of squash of all sizes, shapes and colors, in the fall. When the building itself was expanded several years ago, wood from trees on the Bray property was used in the construction. The ice cream parlor's fireplace was built using stone collected from nearby creeks.

That's right; you can sit by a fire and eat homemade ice cream at Bray's. Flavors include peach, jalapeno peach, chocolate cherry mint, banana, maple walnut, and pumpkin. Many of the ice creams incorporate fruit from the farm. The frozen treats menu also features milk shakes and root beer served in

**Bray Orchards &
Roadside Market**
2580 U.S. Highway 42
Bedford, KY 40006
(502) 255-3607
www.brayorchards.com

May - November
Daily

*Holiday baskets also available in
December.*

Call for seasonal hours.

frosted mugs. Visitors are encouraged to linger with a selection of used paperbacks.

With more than 20 varieties of apples, and just about any berries, beans, tomatoes, squash, leafy greens, cucumbers, eggplant, and peppers you would need to stock your larder, a shopping visit here is always rewarding. But fall may be the very best time at Bray's.

Fall is when the Pumpkin House is on display, a charming hut constructed of straw and wooden shelves which make up the walls when they are lined with pumpkins. Take a stroll in the garden past the pond, and head to the pumpkin patch to select the perfect potential jack o' lantern.

And the best way to cap your visit? With a scoop or two of Bray's homemade pumpkin ice cream, of course.

AYRES FAMILY ORCHARD
Plums and More
OWENTON

The small, tart Damson plum has an ancient history. According to *The Oxford Companion to Food* by Alan Davidson, the fruit is native to Eastern Europe and Western Asia and was known (as evidenced by archeological records) in Western Europe and the Near East from pre-historic times. Its name reflects the history that it was cultivated and exported from Damascus, Syria. Thanks to its astringent flavor, this is not a plum for eating. But it is absolutely perfect for cooking and sugaring to make the excellent Damson plum jam.

While Damson jam was a highly valued addition to Victorian and Edwardian British tables, know that it will not be necessary to employ a staff of downstairs cooks to spend hours cooking up the fruit. Damson plum jam is one of the dozens of jellies, jams, and preserves made from Ayres fruit that's for sale in the farm shop.

That's because Damsons are among the 11 varieties of plums grown by Larry Ayres on his family farm perched on a hilltop overlooking a valley of the Kentucky River.

While Ayres, a retired state forensic biologist, believes that his farm produces more plums than any other in Kentucky, that par-

ticular fruit comprises just part of the bounty found here.

At the end of June, he starts harvesting the first of more than 40 varieties of apples. All fruit is allowed to ripen on the trees for maximum flavor. And his harvest is large enough that Ayres Family Orchard supplies apples to Franklin and Owen County schools, as well as to Jefferson Country Schools (Louisville), the largest system in the state.

Ayres says that Golden Delicious is his best selling apple, but he also cultivates modern varieties such as Cameo, distinguished by a red-striped, rich orange

Ayres Family Orchard
525 Wilson Lane
Owenton, KY 40359
(502) 484-5236
www.ayresapples.com

June - November
 Monday - Saturday:
  Daylight - Dark

skin, and Enterprise, a late-ripening apple that is impressively resistant to a variety of diseases.

No small part of the fun in visiting here is the U-Pick opportunity among the berry bushes and fruit trees that overlook the valley. Peaches, blackberries, and pears are among the other fruits that ripen at different times from late spring until fall.

Be sure to buy some of the Ayres apple cider when it is available. But do know that it is made with much more up-to-date equipment than the antique wooden cider press on display here.

Apple Salad

This recipe is adapted from the one on the Ayres website, which also has recipes for apple butter and apple cake. If you care to, you may also add or substitute grapes, sliced bananas, and sliced celery in this salad.

Salad
8 medium apples (Red Delicious work best)
½ c. raisins
½ c. thinly sliced carrots
½ shredded coconut
½ c. walnuts
½ c. miniature marshmallows

Dressing
Mix together:
¼ c. peanut butter
¼ c. milk or cream
½ c. sugar
½ c. mayonnaise

• Core and dice unpeeled apples and place in weak saltwater to prevent from turning brown.
• Drain apples and add the other ingredients.
• Pour dressing over salad and serve.

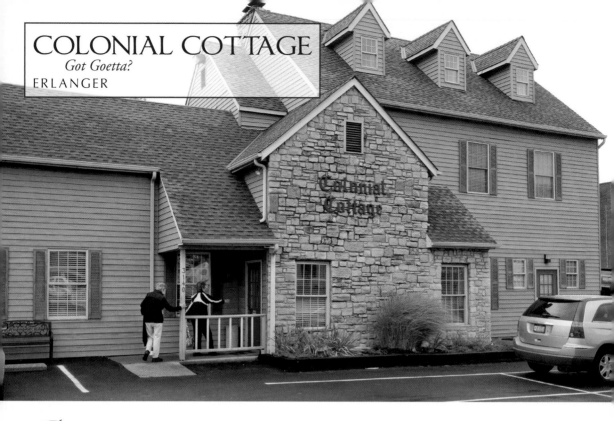

COLONIAL COTTAGE
Got Goetta?
ERLANGER

*P*erched on a slope between a big Kroger-anchored shopping center and busy four-lane Dixie Highway, the Colonial Cottage seems like the architectural counterpart of a boulder left on a flat plain by a retreating glacier. The three story stone house, topped with a row of dormer windows, belongs on the edge of a Bavarian forest, not on a commercial corridor 10 minutes' drive from downtown Cincinnati.

Clara Rich, whose mission was to provide good quality, home-style cooking to her customers at reasonable prices, founded the restaurant in the 1930s. This was, after all, the decade of the Great Depression.

Today, the Colonial Cottage is owned and operated by Matt and Noelle Grimes and the fact that they honor Rich's legacy is apparent in the welcoming atmosphere of the restaurant's warren of cozy wood-trimmed, wallpapered rooms, home-style menu, and prices that remain impressively low. Main courses, with the exception of steaks, are under $20. A remarkable number of items are less than $10.

Signature dishes include fried chicken, country ribs and kraut (remember that Northern Kentucky German heritage), prime rib, country-fried steak, breaded pork chops with cream gravy, and salmon croquets. Lighter fare includes burgers, sandwiches, and homemade soups. Colonial Cottage is also famous for a selection of award-winning cream pies – including lemon and butterscotch – which are baked

fresh every morning and piled high with fluffy meringue perfectly browned on the edges.

Colonial Cottage is also *the* restaurant preserving and celebrating a unique Northern Kentucky/Greater Cincinnati specialty – goetta.

Goetta (rhymes with "meta") is a sausage product of ground pork and beef, spices and oatmeal some-

Colonial Cottage
3140 Dixie Highway
Erlanger, KY 41018
(859) 341-4498
www.thecottageky.com

Monday - Saturday:
  6:30 a.m. - 9 p.m.
Sunday:
  7 a.m. - 9 p.m.

what similar to scrapple. It's prepared by combining the minced meat with steel cut pin oats – the kind used in Scottish haggis, not the rolled oats found in American oatmeal. This mixture, along with onions and spices, is boiled and when cooked, transferred to a loaf pan and chilled. It's served after being cut into slabs and fried.

According to the *Cincinnati Recipe Treasury* (1983), Martha Finke Oehler of Covington claims that her ancestors came up with the original goetta recipe at the end of the 19th century. Certainly, there were many meat-processing plants in the area and the descendants of German immigrants who worked in those plants were happy to stretch their meat with the addition of grain.

Glier's of Cincinnati is the major maker of goetta today (www.gliers.com) and that's the brand served at Colonial Cottage. The Cottage Special breakfast is a filling meal of two eggs, home fries, toast or biscuits (get the biscuits), and goetta or ham (get the goetta). Of course, goetta is available a la carte and as an omelet ingredient. But goetta isn't just for breakfast.

Colonial Cottage also cooks up a goetta Reuben, a goetta burger, a goetta wrap, and even goetta nachos.

Just in case you can't get enough goetta here, know that Glier's sponsors a Goettafest by the river in Newport, Kentucky, every year near the beginning of August (www.goetta.com/en/goettafest/).

Goetta Hash

This is a Colonial Cottage original recipe, provide by owner Matt Grimes.

3 medium potatoes (diced or shredded)
8 oz. goetta (diced or smashed)
¼ c. onion (diced fine)
¼ c. bell peppers (diced fine)
2 dashes Worcestershire sauce
1 dash Garlic powder

- Gently brown goetta, stirring frequently over med/high heat.
- Add potatoes and brown. (Fat from goetta should be enough to allow potatoes to brown. If using a lean goetta add enough vegetable oil to allow potatoes to brown without burning.)
- Remove from heat and combine with remaining ingredients.
- Return to medium heat and cook until vegetables are soft.

Makes about 8 servings.

Leftovers can be stored covered in refrigerator for about 3 days. To reheat, place in a hot skillet with a little fat and add another dash of Worcestershire sauce. Reheat using a lid on the skillet but stir occasionally.

107

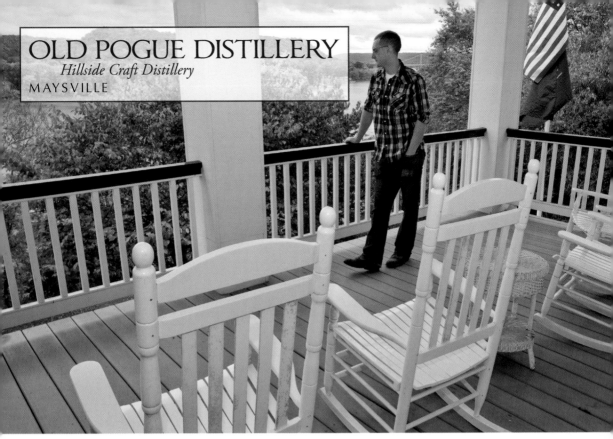

OLD POGUE DISTILLERY
Hillside Craft Distillery

MAYSVILLE

The city of Maysville, originally called Limestone Landing, has an important place in Kentucky bourbon history. In the early 19th century, a section of the state now made up of many smaller counties, was the single, large Bourbon County, which stretched from the Bluegrass Region north to the Ohio River. Maysville was the port from which oak barrels containing corn-based whiskey, stamped with "Bourbon Co." as their point of origin, departed for their long journeys downstream to the Mississippi River and onwards to New Orleans.

The trip took weeks and, as the whiskey sat in the barrels, it took on a reddish hue from the charred oak interiors. (Charring the wood was a time-honored technique for maintaining freshness of water in barrels. French cognac makers stored their distillate in charred barrels so it could acquire color and flavor.)

One idea about how bourbon got its name is that the cognac-loving (but cognac-deprived) French royalist expatriates living in New Orleans favored the "red whiskey" from Bourbon County, Kentucky, and asked for it by name. No one really knows, but it's a better hypothesis than many.

The Pogue bourbon brand dates to 1876 with founder Henry E. Pogue. Only the foundations of the original, very large commercial distillery remain today. Old Pogue is now a craft distillery operation, run by fifth and sixth generation members of the family.

"Our family aspires to make a smooth bourbon," explains sixth generation proprietor John Pogue during a tour of the very compact operation. "Balance is what the Pogues are after."

The family is making bourbon – and rye – in what is certainly one of the most beautiful settings for any distillery in Kentucky. The white brick, antebellum Ryan-Pogue house is set on a bluff overlooking the Ohio. Rocking chairs on the covered porch beckon visitors to sit and enjoy the view. Family distilling memorabilia comprises a mini-museum in rooms on the ground floor.

The distillery itself is in a small building, made of matching white brick, just a few steps

Old Pogue Distillery
716 West 2nd Street
Maysville, KY 41056
www.oldpogue.com
Contact via E-Mail:
  john@oldpogue.com

Tours by Appointment
  Wednesday - Saturday:
  10 a.m., 2 p.m.
  Sunday:
  2 p.m.

from the back door of the house. It contains a Vendome custom-made combination column-pot still, racks containing a few aging barrels (most are stored in rented space with a Bardstown distiller), and a small tasting room and gift shop.

The flagship brand is Old Pogue, a 91 proof bourbon that exhibits a lot of buttered corn on the nose, that same corn spiked with pepper and fruit on the palate, and a smooth, soft, vanilla-oaky finish. While there is no age statement on the bottle, John Pogue said that the bourbon is usually aged between seven and nine years.

The spicy Five Fathers Rye is named in honor of the first five generations of whiskey-making Pogues. Very interesting on its own, it really shines in the accompanying cocktail recipe.

The third product being produced by Pogue is Limestone Landing Single Malt Rye, a clear, non-aged whiskey that shows characteristic rye spiciness. All three whiskies are available for sampling at tour's end and are for sale in the shop.

Travel Tip: Even though the address is West 2nd Street, that's the Exit. Enter from West Germantown Road Route 3056 at the top of the hill.

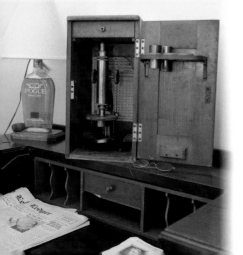

Newport Sinner

Newport, Kentucky, was known as "Sin City" during and immediately after Prohibition. This creative cocktail expression is reflective of the Era it represents: elegant, luscious, and festive. This expression is the creative genius of master mixologists Neal Brown and Adam Hayden of The Libertine Bar in Indianapolis, Indiana, in conjunction with The Old Pogue Distillery.

1 ½ oz. Five Fathers Rye Whisky
¾ oz. Carpano Antica Vermouth
½ oz. Bluecoat American Dry Gin
½ oz. Luxardo Maraschino Liquor
6 dashes Angostura Bitters
Lemon Twist

• Combine all ingredients except lemon twist in a cocktail shaker with ice and shake until thoroughly mixed.
• Pour over ice and garnish with a lemon twist.

ermany might be the predominant European influence in Northern Kentucky, but it's not the only one. Francophiles will think they have stumbled through a wormhole from downtown Maysville to the Boulevard Saint-Germain, when they walk through the tall French doors of the Parc Café, which is, in fact, modeled after Le Procope in Paris. The oldest café in the City of Light, Le Procope was purportedly the first to serve Arabian coffee.

The entrance to the café is off a beautiful stone patio, furnished with umbrella tables and padded benches set into niches in the wall. Colorful flower beds and custom ironwork add to its ambiance as a perfect place to relax over breakfast or lunch in good weather.

The interior could come straight from the *fin de siècle* with tall, tin-pressed ceilings, dark wood trim, a *mélange* of upholstered leather and two-tone wicker furniture, white tablecloths, and bookcases. On weekends, local musicians provide live music.

You can certainly enjoy a first rate cup of coffee or cappuccino or espresso here, along with your breakfast pastries or breads. (It's a happy morning when the cheddar and rosemary scones are available!) As Continental as this all feels,

Chef Barbara Goldman's lunch menu takes full advantage of locally sourced Kentucky ingredients.

Selections change weekly, sometimes daily. The menu is written on a chalkboard behind the display case and counter where patrons place orders. Examples of sandwiches served on a baguette are garlic butter chicken with sliced apples and arugula, kale and prosciutto with goat cheese, and blueberry pecan chicken salad. Curried vegetable, loaded potato, or red pepper Gouda, are some of the soups.

There are always fresh salads and a quiche of the day, as well. Among the former have been sliced pear with blue cheese (optional salmon) and citrus and feta with pickled beets. Country ham, bacon, smoked

Parc Café
35 East 2nd Street
Maysville, KY 41056
(606) 564-9704
www.facebook.com/ParcCafe2010

Monday - Friday:
  7:30 a.m. - 4 p.m.
Saturday:
  8 a.m. - 7 p.m.

salmon, and Gruyere and Swiss are mix and match ingredients that show up in the quiches made with eggs from local farms.

If you just want a small, savory bite, small country ham biscuits are frequently available. Bourbon bread pudding makes a frequent appearance among the dessert selections, as do Italian cream horns and lemon and blueberry tarts. Just as in any good Parisian Café, no one minds if you linger over your coffee and conversation.

Parc's model, Le Procope, has attracted many celebrities, including Voltaire, Diderot, and America's first ambassador to France, Benjamin Franklin, during its long history. Parc Café only opened in 2014, but there is the potential for spotting a famous face.

Nearby Augusta was the hometown of the late singer Rosemary Clooney. (The Rosemary Clooney House on Riverside Drive is now a museum devoted to her career, www.rosemaryclooney.org). Her nephew, actor George Clooney, grew up in the area, too.

Clooney occasionally comes home to visit his parents and there's an unspoken acknowledgement among the residents that no one makes a fuss when he does. With homes in Italy, England, Mexico, and Los Angeles, it's probably a good bet that the star would be attracted to a place like the Parc Café. One can hope, anyway.

BACK ROADS WINE TRAIL

Atwood Hill Winery | Baker-Bird Winery | Camp Springs Vineyard |
Seven Wells Winery & Vineyard | StoneBrook Winery

Scenic Wine Sampling

MORNING VIEW | AUGUSTA | CAMP SPRINGS | CALIFORNIA

Given the fame and success of the West Coast wine making regions in California, Oregon, and Washington, most people don't realize the eastern roots of the American wine industry. The first commercial winery in the U.S. started in Kentucky in the 1790s and, by the middle of the 19th century, Kentucky was the third largest wine-producing state in the country.

The combination of the Civil War, in which many vineyards were heavily damaged, and later Prohibition destroyed the industry. But when tobacco growing declined in the 1990s, farmers looking for new crops and new products started growing grapes and/or making wine. Today there are about 70 wineries in Kentucky and one good way to get a sense of their variety is to travel the Back Roads Wine Trail, consisting of five wineries, each with a different character and its own portfolio of wines.

Visit all five wineries with a Back Roads Wine Trail V.I.P. Passport (available at each) and earn a coaster once you've completed the trail. Tour the trail on Saturday or Sunday afternoons. (Some are open on Friday evenings, too.) Appointments are possible at other times. Call for details.

Atwood Hill Winery
1616 Spillman Road
Morning View, KY 41063
(859) 356-1936
www.atwoodhillwinery.com

Call for details.

Atwood Hill Winery

The western-most winery on the Trail is **Atwood Hill**, owned by Julie and Nelson Clinkenbeard. The farm was established in 1918 and, like so many new wineries, it changed over from tobacco production to viniculture when grapes were planted in 2005. The tasting room is in a charmingly renovated 1930s farmhouse featuring a porch overlooking the vineyards and the forested landscape beyond. A variety of dry, semi-sweet, and fruit wines are made here. A great way to sample them is during the monthly dinners held at Atwood Hill. Call or go online for reservations.

Baker-Bird Winery
4465 Augusta Chatham Road
Augusta, KY 41002
(937) 708-1020
www.facebook.com/
pages/Baker-Bird-
Winery/198129216894848

Call for details.

Baker-Bird Winery

Located just outside Augusta, the stone-constructed **Baker-Bird Winery** looks like it was transported straight from the Rhineland. It's built into a hillside, so when you enter the upper level tasting room, you have no idea that just below is a 90 foot long, 40 foot high wine cellar with a graceful arched ceiling. The weight is supported by the walls which are three to five feet thick. It's impressive, but you may have a hard time pulling yourself away from a chair by one of the gas fireplaces, especially if you have purchased a glass of wine to sit and sip.

Baker-Bird was built by German immigrant Adam Baker and is now

owned by American Dinah Bird, who studied wine making at the University of California – Davis. It is the oldest commercial winery in the United States located on its original site. Kentucky Black Barrel Wine, a Cabernet Franc aged in used bourbon barrels, has won numerous awards. It's more expensive than most Kentucky wines, but oenophiles will definitely want to sample it.

Camp Springs Vineyard
6685 Four Mile Road
Camp Springs, KY 41059
(859) 448-0253
www.campspringsvineyard.com

Call for details.

Camp Springs Vineyard

Vidal Blanc is the premeire wine at **Camp Springs Vineyard**. Its grapes were the first planted, and four wines ranging from dry to semi-sweet to sweet are made from them and aged in either steel tanks or oak barrels. You can try them, as well as seasonal, limited edition fruit wines in the barn-like tasting room.

Seven Wells Winery & Vineyard
1223 Siry Road
California, KY 41007
(859) 816-0003
www.sevenwellswinery.com

Call for details.

Seven Wells Winery & Vineyard

The road to **Seven Wells** is lined with suburban houses, but there's no view of them from the tasting room and its patio overlooking the hillside arbors. Owner Greg Wehman says that his most popular wine is Raccoon Red, a sweet blend of Dornfelder and Chambourcin grapes; it got its name because the biggest threat to the grape crop is – as you may have guessed – hungry, fruit-loving raccoons. But the most interesting wine may be Seven Wells' Noiret, made from a grape developed at Cornell University less than a decade ago. It's a dry and light red with raspberry and peppery notes.

StoneBrook Winery
6570 Vineyard Lane
Camp Springs, KY 41059
(859) 635-0111
www.stonebrookwinery.com

Call for details.

StoneBrook Winery

StoneBrook Winery is a ten-minute drive from Camp Springs Vineyard on a farm owned and cultivated by members of the Walter family since 1871. From blacksmithing to pigs and produce, to dairy and beef cattle, the products have changed over the decades. A 1890s farmhouse now serves as the winery and tasting room, which also features a display of late 19th century farm implements. StoneBrook's grape and other fruit wines have won numerous awards at state fairs and other regional competitions. Check out the much-honored Estate Reserve Vidal Blanc and Cabernet Franc. If you've ever wondered what elderberry wine tasted like, you can satisfy your curiosity here.

117

EASTERN REGION

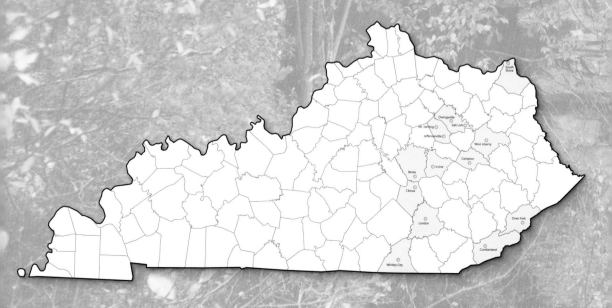

The most rugged terrain in the state is found in the mountains of Eastern Kentucky, most of which are covered in woodland, including the vast Daniel Boone National Forest stretching north to south through 18 counties.

Many of the traditional dishes of the region, such as apple stack cake, date back to the 19th century and involve the use of preserved ingredients. Farming is obviously difficult in the mountainous landscape, but apple and berry growing are increasingly widespread. Historically, vegetables and limited row crops have been grown in hollows between mountains where a few acres of flat land could be planted.

Mountains create pockets of isolation, which also preserves traditions. In this region you'll find historic food landmarks that include one of the oldest operating gristmills in the United States and a 1950s-era diner. Candy is made by hand in a factory using equipment from the early part of the 20th century. There's even a mountain spring where people bring containers to bottle their own water.

Unfortunately, outlets of fast food chains have replaced most of the locally owned eateries in small mountain towns. So many food traditions survive only in private homes and in places mentioned on the following pages.

For a truly unique Eastern Kentucky food adventure, try to get a place on one of Louisville Chef Kathy Cary's annual food tours to the region. The four-day tour, titled "Kentucky…Exploring the Unexpected," takes participants to private farms and homes to experience locally grown food. The tours are limited to 18 persons and take place in June each year. Cary is the owner-chef of Lilly's - A Kentucky Bistro. Call the restaurant to get on an e-mail notification list for registration, (502) 451-0377.

BRAMBLE RIDGE ORCHARD
With a Tea Room, Too
MT. STERLING

A drizzly fall morning is not a great time for working among the trees at Bramble Ridge Orchard, so Terry Peake, who owns and operates the farm with his wife Cindy, is sitting in a corner of the combined farm shop and processing facility, bottling apple cider vinegar aged in used Jim Beam bourbon barrels. He offers tiny paper cups of vinegar to visitors to sample. Tangy, with just a touch of apple and bourbon barrel sweetness, the vinegar's hue is a crystal clear light gold. It is worthy of any recipe calling for the best sherry or champagne vinegars.

The Peakes started their high-density orchard of 23 varieties of apples and peaches grown on 3000 trees in 2001 when he retired from International Harvester and she retired as a professor of education at Eastern Kentucky University.

When school groups are visiting, the farm is bustling with activity, including tours, wagon rides, and a rope maze course. The Peakes keep bees (there's an observation hive) to pollinate the orchard trees and the resulting honey is sold in the shop.

But today is quiet with just the patter of rain on the roof and classical music playing on a radio at one end of the room. While Terry Peake continues to bottle vinegar, Cindy Peake heads to the kitchen to check on the status of dishes she'll cook and serve for lunch. A room to the right of the entrance contains a handful of tables and chairs and is decorated with assorted pieces of china. This is the Green Apple Tea Room, where Cindy serves lunch Tuesday through Saturday, using seasonal ingredients from her garden. But lunch is by reservation only. So please call to book a table.

Inspired by similar little places where the Peakes enjoyed meals on trips to England, its regular clientele come from nearby Mt. Sterling and as far away as Lexington. Since it is both tiny and popular, please be sure to book ahead if you want to enjoy lunch here.

Bramble Ridge Orchard
2726 Osborne Road
Mt. Sterling, KY 40353
(859) 498-9123
www.brambleridgeorchard.com

April - December
  Tuesday - Saturday:
    9 a.m. - 5 p.m.

September - October
  Tuesday - Saturday:
    9 a.m. - 5 p.m.
  Sunday:
    1 p.m. - 5 p.m.

Fried Apple Pie

The shop has plenty of tastes to take home, too. Apples and peaches are sold individually or by the bag. Fresh apple cider, cider slushies, caramel apples, and fried apple pies are available, too. Be sure get a box of apple cider doughnuts. These moist, cinnamon sprinkled delights are made from Cindy Peake's recipe (as are the apple cider doughnuts sold by other Eastern and Central Kentucky orchards). There's an impressive selection of jams, jellies, and butters bearing the Bramble Orchard label, too.

If the day is pleasant, find your way to the porch off of the tea room and relax in a chair with a view of the orchard while you enjoy one of the tasty treats from the shop.

Apple Bread Pudding with Warm Lemon Sauce
Cindy Peake says that this is a favorite dessert in the Green Apple Tea Room.

Apple Bread Pudding
1 c. apple cider
2 c. milk
4 tablespoons butter
1 ½ t. ground cinnamon
¼ c. granulated sugar
Pinch of salt
8 slices of bread or 8 apple cider donuts
3 eggs
1 c. grated fresh unpeeled apple, any variety
¼ c. raisins

• Heat the oven to 350 degrees F. and grease 8-10 ramekins or a large casserole dish.
• Heat the cider, milk, butter, cinnamon, sugar and salt in a medium pan over medium heat until the butter melts, stirring every little bit. Take the pan off the heat.
• In a mixing bowl, tear the bread into small pieces or crumble the donuts. Pour the warm milk mixture over the bread.
• Beat the eggs in a separate bowl and stir in the grated apples and raisins. Gently stir this into the milk and bread until just mixed and pour into casserole dish or spoon into ramekins.

Fresh Warm Lemon Sauce
¾ c. granulated sugar
5 t. cornstarch
Dash of salt
1 T. finely grated lemon zest
5 T. fresh lemon juice
1 T. butter, added after cooking

• Cook over a medium heat stirring constantly until mixture is clear and thick. Then remove from the heat and stir in the butter. This makes about 1 ½ cups of delicious sauce.

Place dish or ramekins into a large pan filled with enough hot water to come up about two inches on the side of the baking dishes. Carefully place this pan into the hot oven. Bake for 45 -60 minutes until a knife inserted in pudding comes out clean. Remove from oven. Serve as soon as possible with warm lemon sauce drizzled over the top.

121

RUTH HUNT CANDIES
Cream Candy, Custom Chocolates & More
MT. STERLING

*B*rowsing the large shop stocked with cases of candy, shelves of gift items, and racks of books, it's hard to imagine Ruth Hunt Candies' modest beginning. Mrs. Hunt, of Mt. Sterling, liked to make candies for her bridge club. Her friends were so enthusiastic about her sweet treats that in 1921 she began selling her confections from her home. By 1930, demand for the candy resulted in the opening of a factory and retail storefront.

Ruth Hunt oversaw the business until her death in 1966, when it passed to her daughter, Emily Hunt Peck. Mrs. Peck sold it to current owner, Larry Kezele, in 1989 and he grew the business to the point where it moved to its current location in 2001.

The company makes about 70 varieties of candy by hand, including chocolates in whimsical shapes such as horses, horseshoes, "Pigs in Mud" (little white chocolate pigs wallowing in a puddle of dark chocolate), and confections customized for weddings and other events. But the staples of the operation are cream candy, bourbon balls, caramels, and the candy bar Kezele calls "a cult favorite in Eastern Kentucky."

Ruth Hunt came up with the Blue Monday candy bar when she was told by a traveling minister who came into her shop that he needed something "a little sweet to help me through my blue Monday." The one-ounce bar consists of a center of pulled cream candy (a Kentucky specialty) coated in a layer of dark chocolate. It's not unlike a room temperature Eskimo Pie.

For something so light and sweet, the making of a Blue Monday requires a lot of muscle. Most of that muscle comes from Candy Chef Junior Carroll, and visitors on a tour of the Ruth Hunt factory can see him in action.

First, the cream, sugar, butter, and water are boiled in a huge copper kettle to make the cream candy, which Carroll pours (using a kettle lift) onto a marble slab used by Ruth Hunt herself. He then proceeds to fold and beat the light brown candy mixture with his hands until it begins to take on the right pliable consistency.

The big lump of candy is transferred to a powered hook where Carroll tends it as it is stretched and pulled, gradually turning from light brown to creamy

122

Ruth Hunt Candies
550 North Maysville Road
Mt. Sterling, KY 40353
(800) 927-0302
www.ruthhuntcandy.com

Monday - Saturday:
 9 a.m. - 5:30 p.m.
Sunday:
 1 p.m. - 5:30 p.m.

white. The candy stiffens so that it can be cut into flat bars, put on a conveyor, and coated in the chocolate.

Demand for Ruth Hunt's signature sweet is high enough that candy is wrapped mechanically. Most of the company's other candies are still wrapped by hand. The original Blue Mondays remain the most popular, but there are also mint (dark chocolate with a mint-flavored cream candy filling) and milk chocolate versions.

A great way to become acquainted with Ruth Hunt's artistry is to buy a box of the assorted chocolates. The company also has a contract with Woodford Reserve to make that distillery's bourbon ball candies. They are a pretty fine introduction to Ruth Hunt's candy-making legacy, too.

In addition to the Mt. Sterling store attached to the factory, Ruth Hunt Candies has a retail store in Lexington at 213 Walton Ave. (859) 268-1559. The company's products can also be found in groceries and gift shops across the state.

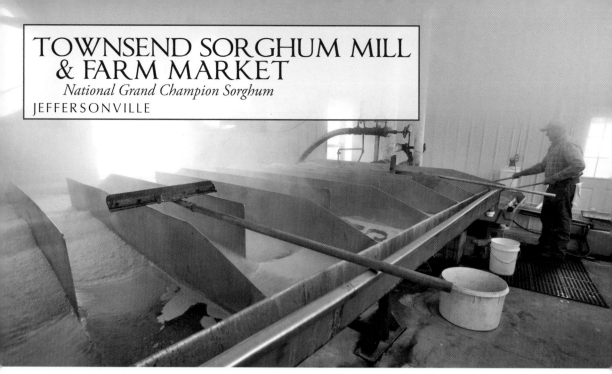

TOWNSEND SORGHUM MILL & FARM MARKET
National Grand Champion Sorghum
JEFFERSONVILLE

$\mathcal{T}$ravel about 12 miles east of Mt. Sterling on U.S. Highway 460 and you'll find Townsend's on the left. In summer and fall, the farm market sells seasonal produce that includes strawberries, peppers, cauliflower, broccoli, sweet corn, watermelon, pumpkins, and more. Gardeners can purchase individual pepper and tomato plants, as well as cold crops – broccoli, cabbage, Brussels sprouts, and their botanical relatives. But the reason most visitors come here is for owners Danny and Judy Townsend's most famous product, sorghum.

Sorghum is a tall cereal grass that can grow as high as 13 or 14 feet. Native to Africa, it is sometimes said to have been brought to America with enslaved Africans. But according to *The Oxford Encyclopedia of Food and Drink in America* there is very good evidence that Benjamin Franklin introduced sorghum to this continent in the late 1700s. While it is one of the so-called "4F plants" (fuel, food, forage, feed), most sorghum grown in Kentucky is used for making a sweet syrup, referred to as "sorghum molasses" or simply "sorghum." (By the way, true molasses is technically a by-product of sugar cane production. Sorghum is the primary reason for processing the plant.)

Since his family has been making it for over 100 years, Danny Townsend grew up making sorghum. He assumed the maker mantle about 30 years ago and, instead of the old-school method of using wood to fuel his steam boiler, Townsend uses natural gas. He says the constant, even heat gives him better control of the sorghum making process and more consistency in his product. He also constantly takes the boiling syrup's temperature, heating it to about 232

degrees F. and cooling it as quickly as possible with cold water. From raw juice pressed from the sorghum stalks to syrup takes about 45 minutes. Eight gallons of juice result in about one gallon of sorghum.

It would be hard to argue with these technological updates. Townsend's Pure Cane Sorghum has been named Grand Champion Sorghum in the National Sorghum Competition. Twice. (Know that sorghum is grown in 28 states, so this is not a limited competition.)

Townsend Sorghum Mill & Farm Market
11620 Main Street
Jeffersonville, KY 40337
(859) 498-4142
townsendsorghummill.com

*Please call for seasonal market hours
Sorghum making in September and
October.*

Even though updates have proved successful, Danny Townsend – a fifth generation sorghum maker, – likes to demonstrate his forebears' methods. Once a year, at the Morgan County Sorghum Festival in West Liberty, he sets up a mill for pressing the stalks; the mill is powered by a mule that walks around it attached to a 30-foot pole. The festival usually takes place on the last weekend of September. Call (606) 743-3330 for exact dates.

Sorghum Whipped Sweet Potatoes

This is adapted from "Molasses Whipped Sweet Potatoes" in The Kentucky Bourbon Cookbook by Albert W.A. Schmid. It simply substitutes sorghum for the molasses. For even more Kentucky flavor, add a splash of bourbon.

3 large sweet potatoes, about 1 pound each
¼ c. sorghum
¼ c. honey
Kosher salt
White pepper
4 T. butter
½ t. cinnamon
⅛ t. grated nutmeg

• Preheat oven to 350 degree F.
• Peel and quarter the sweet potatoes and put them in a roasting pan.
• Pour in 1 cup of water, drizzle the sweet potatoes with the sorghum and honey, and season with salt and pepper.
• Cover the pan with a tight-fitting lid or aluminum foil and bake for about 1 hour.
• Remove the cover and continue cooking for another 30 minutes until the potatoes are dark brown and are tender.
• Remove them to the large bowl of an electric mixer, add the butter, cinnamon, and nutmeg, and mix until all the lumps are gone.
• Pour in as much of the cooking liquid as desired, continue whipping for another minute, check consistency and seasoning (you can add more honey, sorghum, or butter if desired), put the potatoes in a large casserole dish, and serve immediately.

125

GOOD SHEPHERD CHEESE
Pyrenees Style Sheep Cheese
OWINGSVILLE

Many of the world's best-known cheeses, including Feta, Manchego, Pecorino Romano, Ricotta, and Roquefort are made with milk from sheep. One of the lesser-known sheep's milk cheeses is Ossau-Iraty, a variety made for centuries by the Basque sheep farmers of the French Pyrenees Mountains. It is a nutty-tasting, creamy cheese that was eaten mostly within the isolated mountain communities. So it is appropriate that Sanford and Colleen Dotson are raising sheep and producing a very similar, Pyrenees-style cheese on their rolling, 132-acre farm in the foothills of the Appalachian Mountains.

But they are certainly not trying to keep it in the hills.

The Dotsons are the only makers of sheep's milk cheese in Kentucky. So they like to trumpet the virtues of their product. Sheep's milk has only six to seven percent of the fat and twice the solids of cow's milk. This means that there's a greater yield of cheese from the same volume of sheep's milk as cow's milk. Nonetheless, the Dotsons, who run their farm with adult children, Josh and Jenny, have a labor-intensive operation.

They milk their flock of some 80 East Friesian sheep daily, from March to October. Two to three times a week, they use the refrigerated milk to make cheese. It takes about three days' worth of milk (35 gallons), and seven to eight hours of labor (all by hand, no machines), to make seven large wheels of cheese. These are stored in the dairy's cheese cave for two to three months of aging.

Sanford Dotson maintains that his traditional, small batch method has a distinct advantage for making a quality product, "I kinda feel like if you've got your hands in it you can tell what's going on with the

Good Shepherd Cheese
435 Blueberry Lane
Owingsville, KY 40360
www.goodshepherdcheese.com

*To visit, contact via e-mail,
sanford@goodshepherdcheese.com,
for an appointment.*

cheese, unlike factory made cheese. If Americans were eating cheese like this, they would be eating it daily."

He also is convinced that the flavors are more complex when sheep are pasture raised. Being raised in his Kentucky pasture and eating the plants that grow in the limestone soil, also means that even though Good Shepherd Pyrenees Cheese is made from a French recipe, it has a distinctly Kentucky flavor.

Of course, having a flock outdoors near forested mountains populated by coyotes, bears, feral dogs, and other predators, can be a risky proposition. That's why the Dotsons' staff includes several vigilant canines. Australian shepherd dogs, Jim, and Eoghan help move the sheep from the pasture to dairy and back to the pasture. The guard dogs are Maggie (an Anatolian) and Marlee (a Great Pyrenees and Anatolian mix).

In addition to the original traditional Pyrenees Sheep Cheese, Wild Mountain Thyme (seasoned with rosemary, thyme, lavender and other herbs) and Old Smokey (infused with bourbon-smoked peppercorns) are available.

The Dotsons don't have a farm store, but they do sell their cheese online, as well as at the Lexington Farmers Market (p. 26). You can also find it at Lexington's Good Foods Market and at Marksbury Farm Market (p. 46).

SHELTOWEE FARM GOURMET MUSHROOMS
Cultivated and Woodland Fungi
SALT LICK

So much about mushrooms seems magical. They can suddenly sprout in a lawn, often in so-called "fairy rings," right after a spring rain. In folklore and literature they are associated with the uncanny: from the mushroom Alice nibbles at the urging of the hookah smoking caterpillar seated on it, to innumerable associations with elves, pixies, and other supernatural denizens of forests and gardens. Even the common names for many European mushrooms conjure images of the Dark Arts – Corpse Finder, Witch's Hat, Devil's Urn, and Witches' Butter.

Billy Webb, founder and proprietor of Sheltowee Farm, is no sorcerer. In fact, the building next to the one where he grows most of his gourmet mushrooms houses a laboratory stocked with scientific apparatus used to analyze and improve his spore cultures for the USDA Certified Organic mushrooms. Still, there is something a little "other" about his crop. Perhaps it's the sheer quantity and density of the fungi grown in the Quonset hut cultivation building.

Fat cylinders filled with wheat straw, about half the size of a professional punching bag, are sprouting several varieties of mushrooms of all shapes, sizes, and colors. They hang in long rows from a network of metal bars. One 20-pound bag of wheat will yield about six pounds of mushrooms from three harvests over a 60 to 70 day period.

Trumpet-shaped chanterelles with fringed edges, bright yellow oyster mushrooms, aptly-named cauliflower mushrooms which are the size and shape of the vegetable, dark brown shiitakes, light gray Hu mushrooms, and shaggy lion's mane mushrooms are among the fungi growing through holes poked in the plastic casing of the bags. Different mushrooms are cultivated throughout the year, with about 40 varieties in all.

"The lion's manes taste like crabmeat," says Webb. He explains that this particular mushroom is of interest to National Institutes of Health scientists who have done research on nerve-regenerating enzymes they contain.

Webb works his way down a row of bags, using a knife to trim the mushrooms from the plastic surfaces and then

Sheltowee Farm Gourmet Mushrooms
1327 Sheltowee Lane
Salt Lick, KY 40371
(606) 768-9465
www.sheltoweemushrooms.com

Monday - Friday:
By Appointment Only.
Please call.

carefully lays them in waiting boxes. He drives his products to Louisville one day a week to supply restaurant distributors and the city's Whole Foods Market. He makes a similar trip another day each week to Lexington and Cincinnati.

As he puts mushrooms of three different colors into what he calls a Rainbow Box, Webb recalls one of the most unusual uses to which his very colorful mushrooms have been put. "These mushrooms were so pretty that a bride requested 'bouquets' of them as table centerpieces."

By the way, the farm, which is located in the Daniel Boone National Forest, takes its name from the moniker the Shawnee gave Boone. Sheltowee (pronounced she-tah-ee) means "Big Turtle." With a little imagination, some of the rounder mushrooms might resemble the reptiles' shells.

Webb likes to host the occasional school group and educate youngsters about the biology and nutritional value of mushrooms. But the farm is not open for regular tours. Please be sure to call ahead if you want to see how he cultivates his colorful fungi, since this is a very busy and labor-intensive operation. As he says, "I love guests. But I don't like visitors."

Sheltowee Farm Mushroom and Good Shepherd Cheese Tart

This is a recipe from Chef Jeremy Ashby of AZUR Restaurant and Patio (www.azurrestaurant.com) in Lexington for the cooking show he co-hosts on KET (Kentucky Educational Television) called "Food News and Chews." Chef Ashby uses locally-sourced ingredients as often as he can.

1 sheet puff pastry, thawed completely
2 lbs. Sheltowee mushrooms, roughly chopped
5 shallots, julienne
Olive oil
2 T. butter
1 lb. Good Shepherd Pyrenees cheese, grated
2 T. freshly chopped herbs (parsley, thyme, rosemary)
¼ c. local honey

- Preheat oven to 375 degrees F.
- Heat a large skillet over medium high heat; add enough olive oil to lightly coat the entire bottom of the pan. Sprinkle mushrooms into the skillet. Do not overcrowd the mushrooms. If you have to, roast the mushrooms in batches. Brown the mushrooms on all sides and season with salt and pepper. Transfer roasted mushrooms to a mixing bowl for later.
- In the same skillet, after all the mushrooms are roasted, add the 2 tablespoons of butter and the shallots. Cook the shallots on medium heat for 20 minutes until dark brown and caramelized, stirring frequently.
- Add the shallots to the mushrooms in the mixing bowl and stir in the honey and fresh herbs. Season this mixture with salt and pepper and reserve.
- Place puff pastry on the work surface and cut into desired shape. Place the pastry shapes onto the baking tray and par-bake the dough for 10 minutes or until the pastry starts to rise and the edges are just becoming brown.
- Remove from the oven and evenly press down on the pastry to flatten the puffed areas.
- Evenly spread the mushroom and shallot mixture on the tops of the puff pastry. Top liberally with the Good Shepherd cheese.
- Bake tarts again for 10-15 minutes or until cheese is melted and tarts are warm.
- Serve with lots more local honey drizzled on top and some toasted nuts if you like.

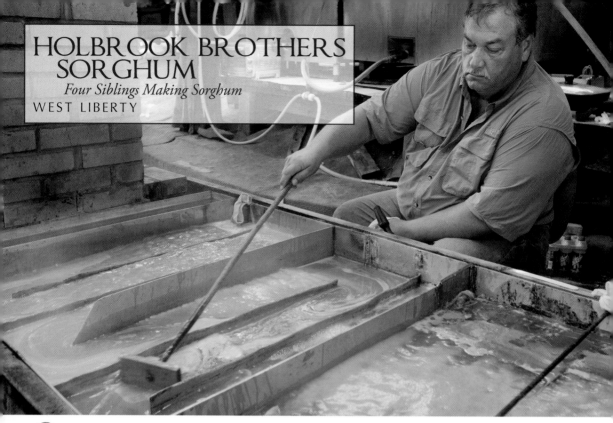

HOLBROOK BROTHERS SORGHUM
Four Siblings Making Sorghum
WEST LIBERTY

On a warm Saturday afternoon in August, the four Holbrook brothers – William, Wendell, Lenville, and Tim – are tending their sorghum operation. This time of year the facility is easy to spot. Several acres of 15-foot high sorghum stalks grow between the highway and the long shed where the juice from the can is being processed into the sweet syrup.

A large conveyer carries freshly cut stalks up to the mill, where they are hand-fed and the juice is crushed from the stalks. The juice that emerges from the mill is pea soup green. It flows into steel evaporation pans where the juice is boiled until it starts to take on a thick, honey-like consistency. As it thickens, it turns a rich golden brown.

When the consistency is just right, a long-handled paddle is used to push it into a funnel where it is filtered into a large container before ultimately finding its way into 16- or 32-ounce jars and plastic jugs.

Dr. William Holbrook, whose veterinary clinic is on the same property as the sorghum plant, explained that his family is relatively new to sorghum. "We started in 1989 with the [Federal] tobacco buyout. Now we make between 1,500 and 2,000 gallons a year, depending on the crop."

They like to have about 1,000 gallons of that yield set aside to take to the annual Morgan County Sorghum Festival (see p. 125). This means the two retired brothers (Lenville was a

farmer and Wendell was a machinist) are stationed at the evaporating trays almost daily. Tim, an engineer, helps out on weekends during sorghum season.

During that season, approximately mid-August until the first killing frost in October, the Holbrooks welcome visitors, which can be individuals, or groups from schools, churches, and other community organizations.

The entire sorghum making process here takes about an hour, from the crushed canes to filtered

Holbrook Brothers Sorghum
78 Veterinarian Lane
  (off U.S. Highway 460)
West Liberty, KY 41472
(606) 743- 3776
www.kyagr.com/KDAPage.
  aspx?id=106,%20

Mid-August until first frost.
Call for information.

syrup. Visitors are each given a Styrofoam cup of sorghum to sample, which is a warm, sticky, very sweet treat, especially when the temperature is cooler than on this day in August. The flavor is reminiscent of dark molasses, but sorghum has a slightly more pungent flavor note. A traditional way to eat it is on fresh-from-the-oven biscuits, often whipped together with butter.

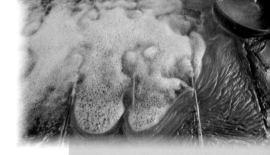

Dr. Holbrook is an advocate for sorghum's status as a natural product. A prominent sign hanging near one of the evaporation trays compares "The Nutritive Values of Several Sweeteners." At 62 calories per tablespoon, it ranks up there with honey. But it also is high in potassium, low in sodium, and even has a little iron. Not to mention that every spoonful is brimming with a Kentucky tradition.

Sorghum Cookies

This comes from Cooking with Chef Joe *by Joe Castro, the former Executive Chef at the English Grill in Louisville's Brown Hotel.*

1 ½ sticks of butter
1 c. light brown sugar (packed)
¼ c. sorghum molasses
1 large egg
2 ¼ c. all-purpose flour
2 t. baking soda
½ t. salt
1 t. ground ginger
1 t. cinnamon
½ t. ground cloves
½ c. granulated sugar

- Preheat oven to 400 degrees F. Line 2 baking sheets with parchment paper.
- Cream the butter and brown sugar together in a large mixing bowl until light and fluffy. Add the sorghum, then the egg, mixing well after each addition.
- Sift the flour, baking soda, and spices together into a medium-size bowl, then stir into the sorghum mixture. The dough will be quite stiff.
- Pour the sugar into a shallow bowl. Form the dough in ¾ inch balls, roll them in the sugar, and place them about 2 inches apart on the prepared baking sheets.
- Bake the cookies in the center of the oven until they are puffed and golden, about 10 minutes. Transfer them to a wire rack to cool.
- Store the cookies in an airtight container. They will keep about 1 week.

Makes 5 dozen cookies.

HOMEPLACE FARM
Seven Acres of Blueberries
SOUTH SHORE

on Davis says that blueberries "are the perfect food." He just may be right. According to the U.S. High Bush Blueberry Council, the tiny fruits are high in anti-oxidants, Vitamin C, manganese, and fiber. And they are low in calories and sodium. Not to mention, they taste great. Historically, American Indians who lived where blueberries grew wild, ate them fresh, but also sun-dried them and to use as meal and to flavor game.

There's quite a bit of history associated with Davis's Homeplace Farm, where he cultivates seven acres of blueberries. His processing facility is in an old church, formerly the Carr Missionary Baptist Church. It was built in the late 1800s on land his great-grandmother donated. Baptisms took place in the Big White Oak Creek nearby. (Davis recalls singing his first song in it at the tender age of one and a half.) The church disbanded in the mid-1990s.

The farm itself has been in Davis's family for generations. He started cultivating blueberries on it in 2002, a few years before he retired from Ashland Oil. By 2006, the berry business was doing so well that the processing had outgrown the family kitchen, so Davis bought the church.

Davis has learned several lessons about blueberry cultivation over the course of the past decade. "Birds used to get about 25% of my crop," he says. So he started covering them. For proper pollination, it's necessary to cultivate several blueberry varieties. These range from Duke (one of the earliest to ripen at the beginning of June) to the medium large Bluejay, and the extra-large, extra sweet Blueray. Each year, to further facilitate pollination, Davis buys boxes of bumblebees. (Honeybees are too inefficient.)

Homeplace Farm
4947 State Route 2070
South Shore, KY 41175
(606) 473-7877

June - July
Please call for hours.

The Homeplace Farm crop is harvested by hand with the help of Don Davis's children, grandchildren and friends. Adding to blueberries' natural health benefits is that no pesticides or herbicides are used here. It's not a U-Pick farm, but customers are welcome to stop by to purchase berries.

Don't be disappointed about not being able to walk along the rows of bushes yourself. A very important "staff member" is Sam the cat, a pale orange tabby who hunts on the property and brings dead snakes to the Davis's back door. Among one of his recent trophies – a timber rattlesnake.

If you can't make it to the farm, know that Homeplace blueberries are distributed to groceries in Louisville, Lexington, Cincinnati, and even parts of West Virginia.

Camille Glenn's Blueberry Sauce

The late Camille Glenn was an acclaimed food writer based in Louisville. She taught cooking classes and contributed many columns to the Courier-Journal. *This recipe come from her* Heritage of Southern Cooking *and is wonderful over pancakes or waffles.*

2/3 c. sugar, or to taste
2 T. cornstarch
Pinch of salt
1 ½ c. water
2 c. fresh blueberries
2 T. butter, melted
2 T. fresh lemon juice
½ t. grated lemon peel

• Mix the sugar and cornstarch together in a medium saucepan.
• Add the salt, water, berries, and melted butter.
• Cook, stirring often, over medium heat until the sauce has thickened and is clear, 20 to 25 minutes.
• Add the lemon juice and peel, stir, and serve.

133

BEREA COLLEGE FARM STORE
Products Raised by Student Farmers

BOONE TAVERN
Historic Hotel and Southern Dining

BEREA

*B*erea College, home to about 1,600 undergraduate students, has a notable history and purpose. Founded in the 1860s, it was the first college in the South to admit students of all races and both sexes. Throughout its history, it has been affiliated with various Christian denominations, but always with an eye to inclusiveness and with a mission to educate the youth of Appalachia and other economically challenged regions. One of the most remarkable features of Berea College is that its students pay no tuition. But they do earn their keep.

In addition to academics, Berea students have traditionally been employed on the campus in a variety of occupations, including as servers, cooks, and housekeepers at Boone Tavern. The hotel has a popular traditional Southern dining room and is listed as an Historic Hotel of America, as designated by the National Trust for Historic Preservation.

(Other such properties include The Bright Angel Lodge in the Grand Canyon and The Plaza Hotel in New York.)

The 63 cozy rooms of the white-columned hotel are furnished with four-poster beds and handsome desks and chairs. Among the most popular dishes on the Boone Tavern menu are chicken flakes in a bird nest, fried catfish with hushpuppies, and shrimp and grits. Kentucky-raised lamb and Bibb lettuce are among local ingredients served here, too. The restaurant's famous spoon bread, a cross between corn bread and a soufflé, accompanies all meals.

Other Berea students learn farming skills. But it's unlikely they will go on to careers with agro-giants such as Tyson Foods or Archer Daniels Midland. Hunt Farm, the college's center of agriculture education, is USDA certified organic. Located on 500 acres sandwiched between the mountains and the

Berea College Farm Store
311 N. Main Street
Berea, KY 40404
(859) 985-3685
www.bereacollegefarmstore.com

Tuesday - Saturday
Please call for hours.

Bluegrass, it contains pastured livestock, gardens, orchards, aquaculture ponds, and beehives.

From hosing down hogs (who cannot sweat) on a sweltering summer day, to planting and harvesting a variety of vegetables, students here are acquiring the knowledge to operate sustainable, and profitable, small family farms.

The bounty from Hunt Farm, as well as other small producers in the region, is sold at Berea College Farm Store and the Berea Farmers' Market. Beans and grains can be bought in bulk. Gardeners can buy a wide selection of seeds. For those less inclined to do-it-yourself, the farm store is simply a great place to enjoy fresh baked goods and a cup of coffee.

Proceeds from all of the Berea College businesses help support the tuition-free status of this historic Kentucky college.

Boone Tavern
100 Main Street
Berea, KY 40404
(800) 366-9358
www.boonetavernhotel.com

Dining Room Open Daily for
Breakfast, Lunch, and Dinner.

Berea Spoon Bread

The famous Boone Tavern spoon bread has been served for decades. This recipe was printed in the Louisville Courier-Journal *in 1951 and reprinted in* The Courier-Journal Kentucky Cookbook, *edited by John Finley, in 1985.*

3 c. milk
1 ¼ c. cornmeal
3 eggs
2 T. butter
1 ¾ t. baking powder
1 t. salt

- Stir meal into rapidly boiling milk. Cook until very thick, stirring constantly as when making mush. Be careful not to let it scorch, which means to stir with vigor.
- Remove from the fire and allow to cool. The mixture will be very stiff when cold.
- Add well-beaten eggs, salt, baking powder and melted butter. Beat with an electric beater for 15 minutes. If hand beating is used, break the hardened, cooked meal into the eggs in small amounts until all is well mixed. Then beat thoroughly for 10 minutes with a wooden spoon.
- Pour into a well-greased casserole. Bake for 30 minutes at 350 degrees F. Serve from casserole by spoonfuls.

SALAMANDER SPRINGS FARM
Sustainable, Organic Co-Op
BEREA

When Susana Lein bought what is now Salamander Springs Farm in the early 2000s, the property was not exactly traditional farmland. Its acres of pure clay were situated on a mountain ridge top. It was a beautiful location, but not traditionally productive.

Lein, who had spent years with Mayan farmers in Guatemala, brought the permaculture practices she had learned from them to her new venture. In the tropics, the organic matter in the soil breaks down very quickly. But it can be preserved if farmers resist hoeing and tilling and let the soil build naturally as plants die and decay.

Lein promotes soil improvement not only by not tilling, but by such simple practices as harvesting a plant by cutting its stem at ground level and leaving the roots to decay and create rich humus. Over time, layers of straw and cardboard (the "lasagna method") are added to fields where they contribute to a mixture of rich organics by hosting a diverse population of microbes as they decay.

Chickens are important partners in soil building. Rather than roaming free, they stay in portable wire pens, which Lein moves around the farm so the birds can scratch and aerate the soil while they feed on weeds.

Since tractors are not used,

Lein can use every inch of arable land on the farm by leaving no space between rows of plants for the machines. This means the look of the Salamander Farms' fields is a little unconventional. For example, 1,200 onion plants grown here are nestled side by side, covering the ground. They look like a large patch of plants growing wild rather than cultivated vegetables.

Actually, just about every aspect of the farm is unconventional. Both the fields of densely planted crops (Lein just scatters seeds, rather than planting rows.) and the surrounding forested mountains are so covered in greenery that there is a sense of rain forest lushness. In fact, she refers to her farm as "a food forest."

Salamander Springs Farm
Clear Creek-Wildie Road
Berea, KY 40403
(859) 893-3360
www.kyagr.com/kdaps age.
  aspx?id=8279

Second Saturday Farm Tours
 April - November
 2 p.m.
  There is a fee. E-mail to book,
  susanalein@yahoo.com.

Water for the farm comes from a local spring. Some of the floors in the buildings are tile made from clay dug on the farm. Salamander Spring is completely "off the grid." All power comes from a solar electric system.

Among the crops grown here are corn, popcorn, beans (pinto, pole, black turtle), pumpkins, squash, carrots, broccoli, lettuce, sweet potatoes, cabbage, daikon, chilies, herbs, and mushrooms. Orchard fruits are dried in a solar powered drier.

Lein offers annual internships on her farm. Participants can learn her intensive, sustainable methods. They either camp in tents or sleep in lofts, use solar heated showers and a composting outhouse, and have light at night from both kerosene lamps and solar powered LEDs. But then working from dawn until dusk, the amount of time anyone would be awake after dark is going to be pretty minimal.

KING BOTTLING
Climax Spring Water
CLIMAX

On a cloudy September day, Bill Shackelford of Livingston, Kentucky has come to the Climax Spring in the Daniel Boone National Forest with his pick-up truck loaded with empty bottles, to fill up on mountain spring water. "We don't use city water," he says. "Coffee tastes terrible with city water."

The free water flowing from a pipe comes from 12 underground springs. They also feed a nearby waterfall. And if you don't quite trust water straight from the ground (though it is naturally filtered both through sandstone and limestone), you can purchase it from King Bottling, which has a modern state-inspected filtering and bottling facility nearby.

David King started the spring water business in 2003. To measure the quality of what he hoped to bottle, King sent a sample to one of the world's largest spring water bottlers, Perrier. Based in France and now owned by the Nestle Corporation, Perrier water is distributed in more than 140 countries.

The Perrier reaction was very positive. Not only did its experts say the Kentucky mountain water "tasted great," the beverage giant made an offer to buy the company. King declined.

A gravity-fed pipe brings water from underground into the King Bottling plant where it is further filtered. Sold under both "Climax" and "Aquaperfect" labels, it is widely available around Kentucky. Most are sold in clear plastic, biodegradable bottles. But around the winter holidays, the water is available in elegant cobalt blue glass bottles.

King Bottling also does about 50 private labels of its water for businesses and institutions such as Woodford Reserve Distillery and Centre College. For

King Bottling
6311 Climax Road
Climax, KY 40460
(606) 256-4142
www.kingbottling.com

Spring open all the time.
Call for plant tour information.

a minimum order of 40 cases, you can even have your own personalized labeling of Appalachian spring water.

Of course, being located in a place called Climax (and no one can explain how the tiny community got its name) provides an irresistible marketing opportunity. Either in the plant gift shop or online, customers can purchase tee-shirts and hoodies sporting the slogan "Have a Climax."

RED RIVER ROCKHOUSE
Hikers' and Climbers' Pub
CAMPTON

*R*ed River Rockhouse owner Aaron Brouwer is a climber. He has spent more than twenty years scaling cliffs from California's Yosemite National Park to Kentucky's Red River Gorge. A few years ago he and his family settled in Eastern Kentucky because, "My daughter wanted to grow up playing in the woods."

He also wanted to open a restaurant that would be the kind of place he and friends would want to hang out in before or after a day on a rock face. That place is the Red River Rockhouse.

In geology, a rock house is a depression in a rock face, not as deep a cave, but deep enough to provide shelter. The Red River Rockhouse, appropriately perched on a mountainside, is a welcome stop whether you have been hiking and climbing or simply touring in this area of natural stone arches and beautiful forests. (Both Natural Bridge State Park and the Red River Gorge are nearby.)

The interior seats about 50, with extra tables on wooden decks outside. Customers can eat at handsome wooden tables and surprisingly comfortable molded plastic chairs, or sink into a comfy leather sofa situated in a shallow alcove off the main dining area.

The menu is relatively short and simple, with lots of egg-based dishes at breakfast (omelets, breakfast tacos, breakfast burrito), and sandwiches and salads at lunch and dinner. But there's an unexpected difference. Brouwer wanted a "simple, approachable, and

Red River Rockhouse
4000 Ky Highway 11
Campton, KY 41301
(606) 668-6656
www.redriverrockhouse.com

Monday & Thursday:
 12 p.m. - 9 p.m.
Tuesday & Wednesday:
 Closed
Friday:
 12 p.m. - 10 p.m.
Saturday:
 8:30 a.m. - 10 p.m.
Sunday:
 8:30 a.m. - 9 p.m.

*Hours vary with seasons, often
shorter in winter.*

delicious" menu, and he wanted dishes made with locally-sourced, often organic, ingredients.

So beef for burgers comes from Marksbury Farm, and chicken is either from Amish farmers or pasture-raised on a farm near Winchester. Flour for pancakes and other baked goods is from Weisenberger Mills. Classic French pastries are baked at National Boulangerie of Lexington. Even the coffee comes from a local roaster, Winchime Coffees in Winchester.

The really good news for the thirsty is that Red River Rockhouse is in Wolfe County, a wet oasis surrounded by dry counties. So it has an excellent selection of micro-brewed beers on tap and bottled, including many from Kentucky. Selections rotate, but Lexington beers, such as West Sixth IPA and Kentucky Ale, are among the regular selections. Soft drinks include Ale-8-One, and Coca Cola bottled in Mexico, which is made with cane sugar instead of high fructose corn syrup.

What's striking about everything is the freshness. Guacamole is made to order. Beef, pork, or chicken tacos are livened with fresh cilantro and lime. Fish tacos are topped with a refreshing mango and cabbage slaw. Slender French fries are addictively good.

Do know that hours are limited in the winter. The Rockhouse is closed through most of December and January, and only open on Saturday, weather permitting, in February and March. So be sure to call ahead if you are planning a visit before the spring thaw.

143

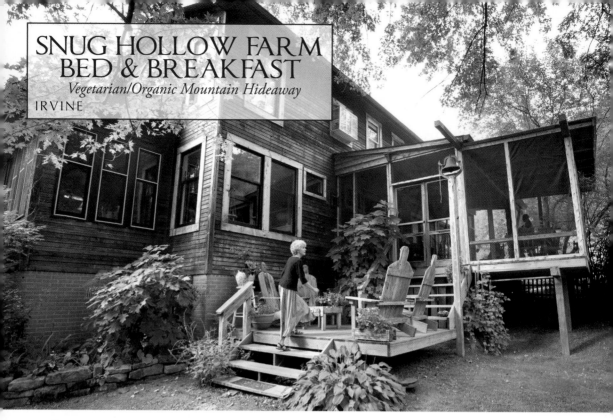

SNUG HOLLOW FARM BED & BREAKFAST
Vegetarian/Organic Mountain Hideaway
IRVINE

The first clue to the peace and seclusion that awaits visitors at Snug Hollow happens during the drive to this idyllic retreat nestled on 300 acres in the mountains. The roads become progressively narrower. The four-lane highway gives way to two-lanes. The two-lane highway becomes a slender winding road with farms on either side and mountains on the horizon. Eventually, you turn up a one-lane road that changes to gravel. (Front-wheel, if not four-wheel drive, will be extremely helpful.)

This gravel drive, lined with dense woods, is the entrance to Barbara Napier's Snug Hollow. It leads to a cluster of beautiful log buildings, including a 185-year-old cabin, set at the edge of a meadow stretching along the hollow between the mountains.

Napier, an energetic sexagenarian with a shock of curly white hair, greets all of her visitors as though they are old friends. (Many are, since they have stayed

here often.) In the hour or so before dinner, guests gather in the farmhouse living room, furnished with antiques and overstuffed sofas and chairs. A large fireplace is ablaze in chilly weather. On a warm evening, rocking chairs on the big porch are a draw.

This could be called "cocktail hour" if Snug Hollow were not located in dry Estill County. While Napier cannot sell liquor, she can allow visitors to bring their own. So be advised that if you want wine to accompany dinner, bring a bottle. (She does have wine glasses.)

The food here matches the comfort, bordering on luxury, of the accommodations. Rather surprisingly, the menu is exclusively vegetarian. But even the most dedicated carnivore will not miss meat. Vegetables come from the Snug Hollow gardens, so meals are freshly seasonal. Okra haters will change their minds about this vegetable when they have it prepared here, served sliced thin and fried in cornmeal. It's as compulsively edible as popcorn. A main course may be vegetarian lasagna scented with just-picked oregano or pasta with greens and sundried tomatoes. Roasted winter vegetables, served with Kentucky bean soup, are a hearty offering, as well.

Whatever the main course, it is almost always served with Napier's aromatic rosemary braided bread. Tip: Don't eat all of it. It makes a great breakfast toast the next morning. On the other hand, breakfast may consist of such de-

**Snug Hollow Farm
Bed & Breakfast**
790 McSwain Branch
Irvine, KY 40336
(606) 723-4786
www.snughollow.com

lights as cherry coffeecake, oatmeal pancakes with gingered bananas, or crispy oatmeal and cornmeal waffles.

All of Napier's baked goods are superb. But for an authentic taste of Appalachia, request that she bake an apple stack cake when you book your accommodations. It's a labor-intensive dish (see recipe), so please give her plenty of notice. Considering that Snug Hollow is usually fully booked months in advance, this probably won't be a problem.

You'll want to stay a few days, not only for the food, but for the wonderful walks through wildflower-filled meadows, relaxing afternoons curled up with a book, and being lulled to sleep at night by the sounds of insects and owls.

While you may feel as though you've made a unique discovery when visiting Snug Hollow, it has been featured in national publications including *National Geographic Traveler* and *Southern Living*. Again, know it is strongly advised to book well in advance.

Dad's Old Fashioned Apple Stack Cake
Reprinted from Hot Food & Warm Memories: A Cookbook from Snug Hollow Farm Bed & Breakfast *by Barbara Napier.*

"Apple Stack Cake is an old Kentucky favorite. Dried apples used in this dessert are usually found in rural Kentucky and are treasures hard to come by. I remember, as a child, kitchens decorated with strings of sliced apples drying in a sunny window."

Cooked Dried Apples
In a heavy saucepan, add 5 cups of dried apples, 1 cup white sugar, 1 cup brown sugar, and 5 cups water. Add spices, such as ground nutmeg, cinnamon and cloves, to taste. Cover and cook over low heat, adding more water as needed. Apples should cook down to a very thick sauce. Stir often to prevent scorching. Let cool.

Stack Cakes
½ c. butter
3 ½ c. all purpose flour
½ c. sugar
2 t. baking powder
1/3 c. molasses
½ t. salt
1 egg, beaten
1 t. ground ginger
½ c. buttermilk
1 t. vanilla

- Cream together sugar and butter; add egg, molasses and buttermilk. Mix well.
- Sift flour, salt, soda and ginger, and add to egg mixture. Mix well and add vanilla. This makes a firm dough.
- With floured hands, pat dough into a 9-inch round cake pan. This recipe should make 6 rounds.
- Bake at 350 degrees F. for 10 minutes.
- When the cake is cool, stack the layers with cooled dried apples. This cake needs to rest for a few hours before serving.

145

APPLE TREE
Apples Grown on Black Mountain,
Kentucky's Highest Peak

CUMBERLAND

Harlan County lies at the heart of Kentucky's coal country and it is home to some of the most rugged and beautiful mountain landscapes in the state. Despite some new transportation construction in the past decade, it can still take hours to drive what looks like a short distance on a map. The roads are narrow, winding, and bounded by mountain faces on one side and shear drops into deep hollows on the other. It is not a place to travel if you are prone to vertigo. But venturing into the mountains here can yield some very interesting food finds.

Kentucky certainly has more than its share of roadside orchard markets but there are fewer in Eastern Kentucky. One of special note is Apple Tree.

Owner Terry Creech used to be a coal miner. Since 1989, he has been a successful apple grower, selling his fruit to the Food City Grocery chain and supplying two school systems in the region. Varieties he grows on eight acres in the valley near his roadside store near Cumberland include Scarlett Gala (a variety patented by his father, J. V. Creech), Jona Gold, Winesap, and Rambo, among others. He also has an orchard planted on a very notable piece of Kentucky geography, Black Mountain.

At 4,415 feet, Black Mountain is the highest peak in the state and it has ecologically unique habitats. Many species of wildflowers, insects, and birds – including the Painted Trillium and Diana Fritillary butterfly – are found here and nowhere else (very rarely else) in the state. Though rich in coal, the mountain is also the focus of vigorous conservation efforts.

Creech's mountaintop orchard yields a unique apple for Kentucky, too. This is the only location in the state where, because of the wide range in temperature between day and night, honeycrisp apples will grow.

Developed at the University of Minnesota as a cold-hearty variety, honeycrisp trees thrive at the high elevation. They are prized for their very sweet flavors and firm, crunchy texture.

It takes almost 45 minutes to travel the 14 miles from the roadside store to a radio tower at the top of the mountain. An ATV is needed to travel for another quarter of an hour up the rutted dirt road to Creech's orchard.

Apple Tree
21991 U.S. Highway 119
Cumberland, KY 40823
(606) 589-5735

August - November
Hours seasonal. Please call.

One would think that transportation is going to be Creech's biggest challenge to harvesting his crop. But, no.

When asked what his greatest problem is growing apples on a mountaintop, Creech has a very simple answer, "Bears."

Black bears, which can weigh up to 500 pounds, are literally a very big problem. And bears *love* apples. But having a bear take a few apples from a tree is not the big deal. When a bear eats a sour apple, one that hasn't ripened, it is not a happy animal. It is, in fact, a very annoyed animal.

"When a bear gets a bad apple, it doesn't just spit it out," says Creech. "He'll get mad and rip the tree, and a few others around it, clear out of the ground."

Keep this in mind the next time you are upset that squirrels are nibbling on your tomato plants.

OVEN FORK MERCANTILE
Historic Store, B&B
OVEN FORK

Continue east on U.S. 119 from Cumberland for about 20 minutes to the tiny community of Oven Fork in Letcher County. On your right, you'll see a derelict coal mine. A Kentucky Highway Historical Marker at the entrance explains that this was the Scotia Mine, where an explosion on March 9, 1976 killed 15 miners and trapped many others. Two days later, a second explosion killed 11 more men. It was one of the worst accidents in coal mining history and the reason, due to the national news coverage, that Oven Fork became a household name at the time. But a positive result of the disaster, caused by safety violations at the mine, was the passage in 1977 of the Federal Mine Safety and Health Act.

Today, if a journalist visits Oven Fork, it will probably be to visit the quaint, almost century-old store, just a few minutes drive further from the mine. Oven Fork Mercantile is a frame and log building with a wide wooden porch out front and a small area to one side with room to park a few cars. Step up onto the boards to the porch and enter the store through the swinging screen door, where you will probably find owner Barbara Church behind the counter.

The wall behind her is lined with shelves holding merchandise and the wooden cubbies that served as boxes from when the store housed Oven Fork's post office. The wooden cubes now hold collectible glasses and mugs.

In an area where there are not a lot of restaurant choices besides fast food outlets, Church offers a ca-

sual alternative. Oven Fork Mercantile is famous in the region for its chili dogs. You can have one with just chili added, or garnished with mustard and onions. The dogs come with a side of slaw. Pulled pork barbecue sandwiches are available, too. Soft drinks and bottled Climax Spring Water are available in a

Oven Fork Mercantile
8494 U.S. Highway 119 South
Oven Fork, KY 40823
(606) 633-8909
www.ovenfork.com

Monday - Saturday:
 10 a.m. - 5 p.m.
Sunday:
 Open at 1 p.m. "Sometimes."
 Call ahead.

small refrigerator. If you have a sweet, rather than savory, tooth, Church also sells several flavors of her homemade fudge.

From the small front room of the store, where the food is served, an opening leads to the warren of rooms that make up the current store. The vintage goods sold here include clothing, toys, costume jewelry, tablecloths, dishes, glasses, and lamps. There's a display of arrowheads and old mining artifacts. Customers can order handmade hickory bark bottom chairs.

"You never know what someone is looking for," says Church. "That's why there's a little bit of everything here."

The building also has a room that Church rents out overnight. It and a couple of other houses that she owns down the road constitute her bed & breakfast business. (Hotel rooms are in short supply around her, too.)

One feature she hasn't mentioned is the artwork on the walls. The paintings are hers. One, of seven soot-covered men who

have just emerged from a coal mine, is especially evocative. It may even seem oddly familiar.

That's because it was used on a set in the FX network's television series "Justified." The series is set in eastern Kentucky, in the region where Oven Fork Mercantile is located, but it is filmed in California. The creators of the series manage some authentic Appalachian atmosphere by using Church's painting. Prints of it are sold in the store.

McHARGUE'S MILL
Water-powered Historic Mill, Corn Meal
LONDON

*L*evi Jackson (1815-1879) was the first county judge of Laurel County, and land that is now the state park was part of a Revolutionary War land grant to his father-in-law, John Freeman. The property was notable for having a tavern that catered to settlers traveling along the Wilderness Road from the Cumberland Gap into Kentucky. The road was paved in the 20th century. Today it is KY Highway 223, some of which runs through the park.

Several log buildings comprising the Mountain Life Museum commemorate this pioneer history. They include McHargue's Mill, a replica of the gristmill that was originally built on this site on the Little Laurel River. As you walk along the path to the mill building, you'll pass the largest collection of millstones in the U.S. Inscriptions on them reveal that many were brought to this country from Europe. Pretty heavy objects to transport across the ocean, but a testament to their importance. Apparently, relatively soft Kentucky limestone would wear too quickly to be much use in grinding meal.

McHargue's Mill isn't just a monument to the past. It is still a working, water-powered mill. Its original wheel, from 1805, hangs on one wall in the building where corn is ground by miller Bob House on Saturdays and Sundays during the summer.

Visitors are welcome to watch the process. House pours corn into a wooden tub where the water-powered wheel grinds it into meal. When the water is low

it can take all day, eight hours, to grind 50 pounds. High water is better, since about 200 pounds can be made in the same time.

McHargue's Mill
Levi Jackson Wilderness Road
 State Park
998 Levi Jackson Mill Road
London, KY 40744
(606) 330-2130
www.parks.ky.gov/parks/
 recreationparks/levi-jackson/

Memorial Day Weekend -
 Halloween:
  Cornmeal ground most
  Saturdays and Sundays.

You can purchase two-pound cloth bags of the cornmeal, to which nothing has been added, including preservatives. House says that it has a shelf life of about two weeks at room temperature and about two months refrigerated. If you still haven't used it by then, you can freeze it and "it will last much longer."

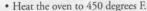

Real Cornbread

Corbin native Ronni Lundy explains in her treasure trove of Appalachian regional recipes, Shuck Beans, Stack Cakes, and Honest Fried Chicken, *that "If God had meant for cornbread to have sugar in it, He would have called it cake." In other words, authentic Southern cornbread, including cornbread from Kentucky, is NOT sweet. This recipe is adapted from Lundy's 1991 cookbook and the instructions assure a great cornbread crust. Fittingly, her family always held its annual summer reunion at Levi Jackson State Park. The cornmeal ground at the park's mill is perfect for this recipe.*

4 T. bacon drippings
2 c. finely ground white cornmeal
1 t. salt
½ t. baking soda
½ t. baking powder
1 large egg
1 ½ c. milk or buttermilk

- Heat the oven to 450 degrees F.
- In a 9-inch round cast-iron skillet (9 or reasonable facsimile thereof), put about 4 tablespoons of drippings.
- Pop the skillet, grease and all, into the oven. (Please note you can't accomplish what you want by heating the skillet on top of the stove. This creates hot spots on the bottom of your skillet, which in turn will make your cornbread stick to the pan.)
- While the grease is getting good and hot in the oven, mix cornmeal, salt, soda, and baking powder in a big bowl. Add the egg and milk, or buttermilk, and stir until just blended.
- Remove the skillet from the oven and very, very carefully (don't burn your hand!), swirl the grease around in the skillet so it coats the bottom and lower half of the sides.
- Pour the hot grease into the cornmeal mix and, if everything is perfect, it will snap, crackle, pop, and bubble invitingly.
- Mix lightly until the grease is just blended in, then pour the cornbread batter into the hot skillet and put it back in the oven for 20-25 minutes until the bread is firm in the middle.
- Serve from the skillet, or turn the skillet upside down over a big plate and the cornbread should slip right out.

DAIRY BAR
50's Diner
WHITLEY CITY

The Big South Fork National River and Recreation Area includes 119,000 acres of wilderness in which the Big South Fork River and its tributaries have carved a series of scenic gorges. It features some 150 miles of hiking trails and 170 miles of horseback riding trails. Fishing and kayaking are popular activities, too.

One of the few towns in the area is Whitley City, where many visitors who have come to the Big South Fork to take advantage of the recreational activities find themselves drawn to a vintage diner. While it isn't dishing up any traditional Kentucky foods, it is a fine example of American food nostalgia.

With its red neon sign and the conspicuous green and white striped awning, the Dairy Bar is impossible to miss. On a busy evening in the summer, cars may be several layers deep in the parking lot, which no one minds because there is 1950s-style curb service. A carhop will come out to your vehicle, take your order, and return with it in a few minutes.

The interior is largely unchanged from the middle of the last century, too. Formica tables, vinyl-covered booths, and even a large poster

of Elvis set the tone. The menu is classic burger and fries fare, plus milkshakes and soft serve ice cream.

While there are a variety of sandwiches, including pork tenderloin and grilled chicken, the specialty of the Dairy Bar is the Dixie Whopper. This is a double decker burger served on a golden toasted bun dressed with shredded lettuce, raw onion, melted American cheese, and pickles. But what really makes the Dixie Whopper special, apart from its considerable size, is that tartar sauce is used in place of regular mayonnaise. This "special sauce" adds an extra touch of flavor.

Recommended accompaniments for the Dixie Whopper are the Dairy Bar's crunchy onion rings and

Dairy Bar
198 South Main Street
Whitley City, KY 42653
(606) 376-2124

Monday, Tuesday, Thursday,
 Saturday:
 8 a.m. – 9 p.m.
Wednesday & Friday:
 8 a.m. – 10 p.m.

one of the milk shakes, available in more than 30 flavors. These range from the traditional (chocolate, strawberry) to the slightly unusual (banana, cotton candy.) If dairy isn't in your diet, the diner has a selection of Pepsi products, too.

Meet me at the Dairy Bar - 1958

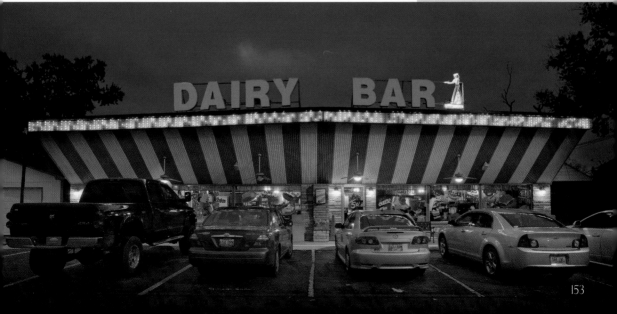

SOUTH CENTRAL
REGION

Bowling Green
Russellville
Austin
Fountain Run

This is the area also sometimes known as Cave Country, since Mammoth Cave National Park, home to the longest known cave system in the world, and other underground attractions are found here. Also of note to tourists is the National Corvette Museum just off Interstate 65 at Bowling Green.

Many of the farmers of South Central Kentucky have ties to markets in Tennessee, as well as to their home state. For that reason, cheese, organic milk, pasture-raised beef and other goods from the region can be found on store shelves in Nashville, as well as in Kentucky cities. Obviously, from this list of products, cattle are the most important livestock. The region's rolling green pastures are as populated with beef and dairy cattle as the Bluegrass is with horses.

KENNY'S FARMHOUSE CHEESE
Artisan Cows' Cheese
AUSTIN

A little over 20 years ago, Kenny Mattingly came to an unpleasant realization about his family dairy farm. His 120 head of cattle were producing plenty of milk, but the price of milk had fallen dramatically. The cows simply were not going to support the farm. So Mattingly started to look for a way to make the cows pay.

He took a trip to Europe to find out how small family farms similar to his were surviving, even thriving. "That's when I discovered that I needed to find a way to 'add value' to what I already had," Mattingly recalled. What he decided to do was experiment with making cheese.

But to make cheese, he needed specialized equipment. He found a person who had equipment to sell,

since she was retiring. But when he approached the bank for a loan, he was turned down. "So I paid installments of $300 a month until the equipment was paid for."

It was 1998 and Mattingly started with Gouda. He made 4000 pounds of cheese that year. In 2014, Kenny's Farmhouse Cheese was available in almost 40 varieties including Brie, three flavors of Asiago, half a dozen versions of Cheddar, Kentucky Bleu, flavored Monterey Jacks (regular, chive-onion, garlic-paprika, jalapeno), Havarti, Mozzarella, Colby, Swiss, and more. Altogether they added up to 140,000 pounds sold.

Kenny's Country Cheeses are finding markets in Chicago, Atlanta, and other big cities. And Mattingly's biggest customer is Creation Gardens, a Louisville-based food distributor, which is why Kenny's Cheeses can be found in groceries all over Kentucky, as well as on menus in many, many restaurants. Cheese lovers are welcome to visit the farm six days a week for tours and tastings.

Four of those days find Mattingly in the cheese-making room. Milk is piped straight from the dairy, just a few hundred feet away. It's hard to imagine how a product could be any fresher. Visitors can watch through a glass window as Mat-

Kenny's Farmhouse Cheese
2033 Thomerson Park Road
Austin, KY 42123
(270) 434-4124
www.kennyscheese.com

Monday - Friday:
9 a.m. - 4 p.m.
Saturday:
11 a.m. - 4 p.m.

Please call in advance for a tour. There is a charge for groups of 10 or more.

tingly, wearing a hairnet and rubber apron and boots, stirs milk to cool it after pasteurization. He then adds rennet (a complex of enzymes) that begins the process of turning the milk into cheese. The mixture starts to thicken and he patiently stirs, and then rakes the contents of the trough until he has a product ready for the aging room.

The shop in the front of the dairy sells all the varieties of cheeses, as well as gift baskets.

Demand has been such for Kenny's Farmhouse Cheese that the herd now numbers about 145 head. Breeds include Holstein, Jersey, Brown Swiss, and Norwegian Red. The Mattingly cows that roam the farm's pastures are not given synthetic hormones, and enjoy corn and hay raised on the farm to supplement their pasture grazing.

Cheeses are aged, packaged and shipped in the same facility where they are made. Mattingly's 11 employees, who between them have a payroll of about $300,000, carry out all this work.

Mattingly smiles when he says that the bank that wouldn't give him a loan for his first equipment is now more than eager for his business. "It's amazing what little farms can contribute to the local economy."

Weisenberger Stone-ground Grits with Kenny's Gouda

This is a little different from the recipe for cheese greats from Weisenberger Mills, even though it also uses Weisenberger's grits. It was printed in the Louisville Courier-Journal on 19 August 2011, and comes from Lelia Gentle, a former restaurant owner and now proprietor of Dream Catcher Farm, which produces pasture-raised beef sold at Louisville area farmers' markets. Her advice about the recipe: "Grits are a great side item for any breakfast menu. But it can also be used as the main attraction. Add any seasonal grilled or sautéed vegetable or your choice of local meats, such as bacon or sausage."

2 c. water or vegetable stock
2 c. milk
1 c. stone-ground grits
1 T. butter
4 oz. Kenny's Gouda cheese, grated
1 ½ t. salt
½ t. pepper

- Bring stock and milk to a boil. Turn down to low, and slowly whisk in the grits. Cook, stirring occasionally, for about 40 minutes.
- When grits are done, add butter, cheese, salt and pepper. If grits are too thick, you may thin with a little more milk or cream.

Serves 6.

157

DOWNING CATTLE COMPANY
Pasture Fed Beef and Pork
FOUNTAIN RUN

When Jeff Downing was in grade school, his dad decided to supplement the family farm's business by building a meat processing facility on the property. He was meeting a demand from his livestock-raising neighbors for a place nearby at which to slaughter cattle and hogs and butcher their meat.

Almost half a century later, Downing Cattle Company happens to have all the elements to meet a growing demand for pasture-raised, hormone- and antibiotic-free meat, which is not just a desire of nutritionally conscious and eco-savvy city-dwellers.

"We felt like there was a market and more people were getting concerned about where their food was coming from and this gave them the option. Yes, we do have customers who purchase our meat because of this," says Jeff Downing's wife, Melinda.

The farm had always had cattle and, as was true throughout so much of Kentucky, tobacco. The Downings had intended to condition cattle for feedlots, but found their niche market instead.

Today, the Downings raise Black Angus beef cattle and they process and sell pork from their neighbor, John Harlin, who raises all-natural Yorkshire pigs on his farm in Bugtussle. (No, this is *not* a fictional place name.) As with the Downings' cattle, Harlin's pigs are pasture raised and fed locally-grown grain as a supplement when fields are winter brown.

Customers are welcome to visit Downing Cattle Company to purchase meat. It can also be found at Flapper's Market (Fountain Run, KY), Sheryl's First Stop (Gamaliel, KY), Amos Grocery (Amos, KY), Hendersonville Produce (Hendersonville, TN), The Produce Place and Good Food for Good People (both in Nashville, TN).

Downing Cattle Company
405 Circle D Lane
Fountain Run, KY 42133
(270) 434-2559
www.downingcattlecompanyinc.com

Thursday - Friday:
  8 a.m. - 5 p.m.
Saturday:
  8 a.m. - 12 p.m.

Among area restaurants serving Downing meats are Nannie Jo's Country Cooking in Fountain Run, Marie's Drive Thru in Tompkinsville, and Fido's Restaurant in Nashville.

Given family involvement in The Downing farm, their pasture-raised meat will probably be available for years to come. Working alongside Jeff and Melinda Downing are their son Will and his wife Bethany, plus their niece Clara Howser.

Melinda Downing affirms this family commitment, "We welcome everyone to come and visit. The cattle and the processing facility are on the same farm. We are USDA inspected and have an inspector with us everyday. We strive for a good quality product that we would, and do, eat ourselves."

Beef Fajitas

This is Melinda Downing's method for making fajitas. Figure portions on whether you want to make a little or a lot.

Flank Steak
Your favorite fajita seasoning
Your favorite vegetables
Tortilla chips or rice
White cheese dip

- Slice flank steak very thin across the grain.
- Add your fajita seasoning and mix well with meat, and place in a heated skillet.
- Add sliced onions, sliced green peppers, mushrooms and tomatoes. Cook until meat is tender; do not overcook.
- Add meat to tortilla chips or rice and cover with white cheese dip.

CORSAIR DISTILLERY
Unusual Craft Spirits
BOWLING GREEN

A "corsair" is, of course, a pirate. Consider the styles of spirits being distilled at Corsair, housed in a refurbished former department store in downtown Bowling Green, and you may think someone hijacked the operation.

Triple Smoke Whiskey uses three fractions of malted barley and smokes each over a different combustible. One part is smoked with peat, certainly not unheard of in Scotch circles. But the other two portions are smoked over cherry and over beechwood.

Then there's the absinthe. That's right, the notorious liquor of Belle Epoque, Paris. In addition to wormwood, Corsair's is flavored with tarragon, citrus, and red hibiscus, which turns it bright red.

Gin and spiced rum are distilled with sustainably harvested botanicals. Fair trade whole bourbon vanilla beans give the vanilla vodka its punch. And since Corsair is all about innovation, one of its flagship whiskies is distilled from quinoa. That's right. White and red versions of the trendy "power grain" are used with malted barley to make quinoa whiskey.

A tour of the Kentucky distillery (Corsair also has a facility in Nashville that brews beer as well as distills spirits) reveals much else that is unique, even in the craft spirits industry, which has more than its share of experimental distillers.

The tasting bar and shop occupy a relatively small area at one end of a block-long space. Old brick walls have been exposed and wood flooring has been restored. Groupings of sofas and chairs are scattered about, since Corsair rents this out as an event space.

In contrast, the distillery seems tiny. Steve Whitledge, assistant distiller, explains on a tour that the 50-gallon pot still was custom made to Corsair's specifications by Vendome Copper & Brass Works of Louisville. It is equipped with a vapor basket – a fat stainless steel cylinder connected to the neck of the pot still – that allows the infusion of aromatics and spices. These are kept in rows of jars on shelves taking

Corsair Distillery
400 East Main Avenue
Bowling Green, KY 42101
(270) 904-2021
www.corsairdistillery.com

Tuesday - Thursday:
11 a.m. - 5 p.m.
Friday - Saturday:
11 a.m. - 6 p.m.

up one corner of the room so varied and multicolored that they look more like they belong in a bakery (or an alchemist's lab) than a distillery. Racks of barrels of aging spirits, the bottling equipment, and boxes of labels occupy the same space.

Derek Bell and Andrew Webber are the founders of Corsair, which got its start in Bell's garage. Odd as some of their experimental spirits may seem (buckwheat and malted oats are other grains that have appeared in Corsair distillations), they are obviously doing something right.

The distillery has won more than 40 metals in national and international spirits competitions. And *Whisky* magazine, published in Britain, has named Corsair both "American Whiskey Brand Innova-

tor of the Year" and "American Craft Distiller of the Year." Not bad for an operation that has only operated at its current site since 2013.

Dark as Night Cocktail
The combination of absinthe and coffee may well give new meaning to DuPont's "Better Living Though Chemistry" catchphrase!

2 oz. absinthe
2 oz. coffee
¼ oz. simple syrup
Lemon twist

• Combine liquid ingredients in a rocks glass with ice. Stir.
• Garnish with the lemon twist.

Chaney's address may be Bowling Green, but the restaurant and its adjacent dairy farm are several miles from the city. And while it has a conspicuous location at the corner of Highway 31W and South McElwain Road, the setting is decidedly rural. Surrounded by flat farmland planted in corn, soybeans and other crops, only silos and barn roofs interrupt the horizon.

The restaurant portion of the operation is built to resemble a barn with lots of wood siding and even a resident life-sized model cow. A gift shop at the entrance is the kind filled with all kinds of stuff, from tee-shirts to candles, that no one actually needs, but are fun to browse through, and perhaps even purchase, anyway.

Plenty of visitors come to Chaney's just to enjoy the sandwich-based menu. The counter where you place your order is "overseen" by the model cow that provides the perfect photo op for children (or adults) who might be shy around her living counterparts, found in residence at the dairy farm only a few hundred yards away. Specialty sandwiches include the Dairy-Aire (pimento cheese made from a family recipe) and the bestselling chicken salad, dubbed The Grand Champion.

Potato soup is available very day. Other homemade soups are offered on a rotating basis and include broccoli cheese, chili, white beans and chicken, and vegetable beef.

But this is Chaney's *Dairy* Barn, which means the specialty of the house is rich, decadent, homemade ice cream. Naturally, there's a much longer list of ice cream flavors than sandwiches, soups, and salads combined. A generous scoop (or two) makes a great lunch. Honest.

Over 35 flavors are offered, though some only seasonally. In addition to the standard vanilla, chocolate, and strawberry, look for Chaney's specialties such as banana, toasted coconut, peach, cinnamon, hazelnut, mint chocolate chip, bourbon vanilla bean, Cow Tracks (vanilla with Snickers candy bar pieces and caramel swirl), Big Red Rumble (choco-

**Chaney's Dairy Barn
& Restaurant**
9191 Nashville Road
(U.S. Highway 31W)
Bowling Green, KY 42101
(270) 843-5567
www.chaneysdairybarn.com

Monday - Thursday:
  10 a.m. - 8 p.m.
Friday - Saturday:
  10 a.m. - 9 p.m.
Sunday:
  12 p.m. - 8 p.m.

Closed in January.

late with red velvet cake pieces), and orange juice sherbet (not just for breakfast).

Peach is offered in the summer and pumpkin is available in the fall.

Ice cream isn't the only attraction for youngsters. A playground behind the restaurant features a giant slide, a swing set, a huge sand pit, and a multi-colored jumbo jumping pillow which looks like a giant roll of Life-Savers imbedded in the ground.

Visitors to the playgrounds can see the dairy farm and its herd of resident Jerseys in the near distance. Farm tours are available April though October for a small fee, but you need to have a minimum of ten in order to go on one. Held at 9 a.m. and 10:15 a.m., they are geared toward groups with children and include a wagon ride from the restaurant to the farm's barn, a milking demonstration, the opportunity to pet a calf, and not-surprisingly, a scoop of ice cream.

Chaney's offers another favorite family activity on summer evenings. Everyone is encouraged to bring a folding chair or blanket to enjoy an outdoor movie. One side of the barn serves as the screen.

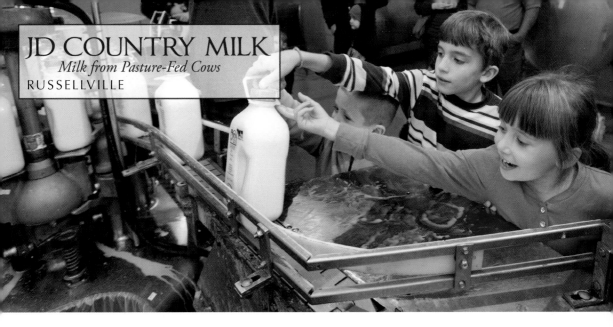

JD COUNTRY MILK
Milk from Pasture-Fed Cows
RUSSELLVILLE

The message on the side of a bottle of JD Country Milk clearly states the philosophy of Willis and Edna Schrock and their eight children, the proprietors of JD Country Milk:

"Our family is committed to providing you with quality, all natural, farm fresh milk. Our cows are free to roam on green pastures of chemical-free grass. We pledge to treat our cows with respect. Happy Cows produce Healthy Milk."

One of these happy cows, Bossy, was on hand meeting and greeting visitors during the annual JD Open House, which usually takes place the last Saturday of October or the first Saturday of November. While Willis Schrock held her halter, children took turns petting her nose and flanks and even sitting on her back. Bossy was completely unfazed by the attention.

In addition to getting acquainted with Bossy, customers and neighbors can watch the bottling operation and enjoy a buffet lunch, accompanied by glasses of the Schrocks' milk or steaming cups of hot chocolate.

JD Country Milk is sold as whole, two percent, skim, and chocolate. The company also makes liquid yogurt. Why all the fuss over this particular milk?

It's a notable product of traditional (the Schrocks are Mennonites) and modern dairy methods. With a grant from the state, the family outfitted their operation with state-of-the-art bottling equipment. While using this technology, they strive to preserve the natural, sweet taste of milk by pasteurizing it at a lower temperature than that employed by big, com-

mercial dairies. Pathogens are still killed, but many of the enzymes in milk are not denatured at this temperature and are still active.

Many customers perceive this as being healthier than most milk found on store shelves. It tastes better, too.

164

JD Country Milk
1059 Ellis Road
Russellville, KY 42276
(270) 726-2200
www.jdcountrymilk.com

Tuesday - Friday:
 8 a.m. - 5 p.m.
Saturday:
 9 a.m. - 3 p.m.

The milk is not homogenized, so there's still a little taste of the cream fraction that naturally occurs in fresh milk, which contributes to the flavor. And there's another traditional touch – JD Country Milk is sold in returnable glass bottles, not cardboard cartons.

The Schrocks barely keep up with demand from customers in Nashville, Lexington, and Louisville, where is it sold at the Whole Foods Markets in those cities, as well as other outlets. Specialty markets on smaller cities, including Bowling Green and Owensboro, carry the milk, too.

Given this demand, the Schrocks are acquiring a herd of their own, so there may be a tour of the cow sheds, as well as the bottling plant, by the open house of 2015.

Meanwhile, the other words of wisdom printed on the JD Milk bottle: "Milk puts you in a better MOOOOOOD!"

Hard to argue with that after a visit to, and a glass of, JD Country Milk.

WESTERN REGION

- Owensboro
- Utica
- Sturgis
- Madisonville
- Dawson Springs
- Princeton
- Kuttawa
- Benton
- Aurora
- Hopkinsville

The geography of the western portion of Kentucky is strikingly different from the rest of the state. There are forests, but the region is notable for an abundance of water in the form of natural wetlands and two enormous lakes. Kentucky Lake (160,300 acres) and Lake Barkley (58,000 acres) were created by the impoundment of the Tennessee River and Cumberland River, respectively. Plus, the Ohio and Mississippi Rivers mark two of the three boundaries with other states at this end of Kentucky. Near their shorelines, much of the land flattens into fields that would look right at home in Kansas.

The presence of all this water may explain one of the region's popular dishes, fried catfish. But for foodies, Western Kentucky means *meat*. Barbecue (all types, but mutton is the regional specialty), burgoo (a meaty stew), and country ham (smoke and salt-cured) are the dishes to seek out.

Mutton is defined as a sheep, ewe or castrated ram, at least one year old. The meat is strong, but stunningly flavorful, and barbecued mutton is found at only a handful of places in Kentucky, mostly in the west.

The origins of burgoo are just about as mysterious as those of bourbon. Sometime in the 1800s it was the name given to a frontier stew that incorporated an array of whatever game and domestic meats were available, including squirrel, venison, pork, chicken, beef, and mutton. (Squirrel has pretty much vanished from modern versions.) Garden vegetables round out the burgoo recipe and include – but are not limited to – potatoes, onions, okra, carrots, and corn.

Once upon a time all American ham was "country ham," as Alan Deutschman explains in his splendid essay, "A Jewish Yankee's Quest for the Last Great Country Hams in Western Kentucky" published in *Cornbread Nation 5: The Best of Southern Food Writing*.

"Farmers killed their hogs in early winter. They didn't have refrigeration, but the cold weather kept the meat from spoiling. Farmers cut off the hind legs of the hogs and rubbed them with salt (as a preservative) and sometimes also sugar (as a tenderizer) and black pepper (an insect repellant as well as a seasoning.) Then they hung these pig haunches from the rafters of a tightly sealed, windowless shack. For several weeks, they left a pile of hickory shavings smothering below."

For immersion experiences in Western Kentucky cuisine, know about three annual celebrations. The Green River Catfish Festival takes place in Morgantown in July, www.morgantown-ky.com/events/catfish-festival/. Burgoo and barbecue are on display in May in Owensboro at the International Bar-B-Q Festival, www.bbqfest.com. And Cadiz is the site for the Trigg County Country Ham Festival every October, www.hamfestival.com.

Here are places to find all of these delicacies, plus a few other uniquely Western Kentucky treats.

MILLER HOUSE
Traditional Dining & A Wall-of-Bourbon Bar
OWENSBORO

*L*ocated on the southeast edge of Owensboro's downtown historic district, the Miller House offers Southern infected dining in an elegant artificial stone mansion (the blocks were constructed in molds with river sand) built in 1905. Tables are scattered through a warren of rooms, both downstairs and up. It's also possible to take advantage of good weather and eat on the front porch supported by wide Corinthian columns, or the side patio, which offers a great view of the house's handsome exterior.

Starters include fried green tomatoes, bacon and grits fritters, and garlic-baked oysters. Salads are included with entrees and all dressings, including the excellent warm bacon vinaigrette, are made in-house. The chicken entrée is served with a savory leek bread pudding. Among the most popular entrees are a coffee and chili rubbed ribeye steak and a seared walleye pike filet served with Brussels sprout slaw.

Accompanying all dinners is a basket of warm sweet potato biscuits, slathered with butter. That's a good reason to look at what's called the "lighter side" of the menu. It includes the Miller House signature shrimp and cheddar grits.

Traditional sweets, such as red velvet cake, anchor the dessert menu. But you may want to repair to the inviting bar in the cellar for an after dinner bourbon instead.

Miller House
301 East 5th Street
Owensboro, KY 42303
(270) 685-5878
www.themillerhouserestaurant.com

Tuesday - Friday:
  11 a.m. - 9 p.m.
Saturday:
  5 p.m. - 10 p.m.
Sunday:
  11 a.m. - 2 p.m.

Dubbed "Spirits," the cozy room of exposed brick and polished wood has not one, but two walls covered in shelves stocked with more than 300 bourbons and other whiskies chosen by owner and bourbon enthusiast Larry Kirk. It should be on every serious bourbon aficionado's list of must-visit bars.

Happily, there are handy leaflets listing all the whiskies and their price ranges placed throughout the room and on the bar. Do be sure to ask about the exact price for a pour from the $20+ listing, since the rare bourbons can be $80 or even over $100 per shot. Yes, you can find Pappy Van Winkle here and not just one expression, but 10-Year-Old, 15-Year-Old, 20-Year-Old, and the 23-Year-Old. Annual releases of the almost as rare George T. Stagg are available from 2011 to 2014.

But you don't have to pay a small fortune to sample some excellent and unique bourbons. Members of the knowledgeable staff regularly venture to distilleries to make selections of barrels from private house bottlings. These are noted in red on the list and include barrel strength Four Roses, 12-Year-Old Elijah Craig, Eagle Rare, Knob Creek, and Henry McKenna, all for under $15 per serving.

MOONLITE BAR-B-Q
Famous Barbecue Buffet
OWENSBORO

*M*oonlite Bar-B-Q is the best-known barbecue restaurant in Kentucky, having been featured in both state and national publications, including all major Kentucky newspapers, *USA Today*, *Southern Living*, *Gourmet* and more. Moonlite's journey to fame began in 1963 when Catherine and Hugh "Pappy" Bosley bought it with a $5,000 down payment they raised from the sale of their home. The restaurant only had 30 seats. Today it has 350. Seating capacity isn't the only large feature of Moonlite.

Thanks to its famous buffet, Moonlite is the favored barbecue joint of those with outsized appetites. Priced just under $11 at lunch and at about $15 and $18 at dinner (higher tariff on Friday and Saturday), it offers a staggering array of meat, vegetables and desserts.

Since it's hard to know what to try, try it all. Just take samples on your first go around. Pork ribs, pulled pork, pulled chicken, sliced or chopped barbecued beef, barbecued ham, fried chicken livers and gizzards, and – the Owensboro specialty – chopped or pulled barbecued mutton. (Moonlite reportedly cooks and sells about 10,000 pounds of mutton every week!)

There's an enormous salad bar that rivals the selection of meats. Hot sides include macaroni and cheese, mashed potatoes, potato salad, and cheesy broccoli casserole, Southern style green beans, white beans with ham, and that other Owensboro specialty, burgoo. Soak up sauces with rolls or corn bread muffins.

Don't forget dessert – lemon pie, coconut pie, peanut butter pie, pecan pie, chocolate pie, seasonal fruit cobblers, and more. Soft drinks and bottled beers are available. But really, who would have room for beer here?

Just in case you find yourself at Moonlite and you do not have the appetite of a 300-pound linebacker, there's also a menu for mortals. A cup of the mutton-

Moonlite Bar-B-Q
2840 West Parrish Avenue
Owensboro, KY 42301
(270) 684-8143
www.moonlite.com

Lunch
  Monday - Saturday:
    11 a.m. - 2 p.m.
Dinner
  Monday - Thursday:
    4 p.m. - 9 p.m.
  Friday - Saturday:
    3:30 p.m. - 9:30 p.m.
Sunday Brunch:
  10 a.m. - 3 p.m.

based burgoo – which is sold by the can or the gallon in the on-site store – is an excellent prelude to a sandwich made with any of the aforementioned meats. Dinner plates include a choice of two sides.

And if you want to throw a party in your backyard, everything on the menu and in the buffet is available for carryout by the pound.

Moonlite can serve up this barbecue bounty because its operation includes its own meat processing plant, which the owners estimate uses about 10% of all the mutton produced in the United States. The open pit, where all the meats are smoked and cooked, are topped with 24 foot long grills.

Even if you can't pay a visit to the Moonlite dining rooms, you can still find burgoo and barbecue sauces in stores throughout Kentucky, Indiana, Tennessee and Ohio. You can also shop online at the Moonlite website for meats and more.

Moonlite's Burgoo

This classic recipe comes from the 1988 edition of The Moonlite Bar-B-Q Inn Collection of Recipes.

4 lbs. mutton
1-3 lbs. whole chicken
¾ lb. cabbage, ground or chopped fine
¾ lb. onion, ground or chopped fine
5 lbs. potatoes, peeled and diced
2 17-oz. cans of corn or 2 c. fresh corn
¾ c. tomato catsup
3 10 ¾-oz. cans tomato puree
Juice of one lemon
¾ c. distilled vinegar
½ c. Worcestershire sauce
2 ½ T. salt
2 T. black pepper
1 t. cayenne pepper (more if you like)
Water
(Some area cooks add dried or lima beans, tomatoes, and a little boiled shredded beef or wild game.)

- Boil mutton in enough water to cover. Cook under tender, about 2-3 hours. Throw out broth and bones. Chop meat fine. Set aside.
- Boil chicken in two gallons of water in a large kettle until tender. Remove chicken.
- Add potatoes, cabbage, onion, corn, catsup and 1 gallon of water to chicken broth. Bring to a boil.
- Meanwhile, chop chicken meat and discard bones and skin.
- When potatoes are tender, add chicken, mutton, lemon, salt, pepper, Worcestershire sauce, vinegar and puree.
- Let this simmer for 2 hours or longer, stirring occasionally as it thickens.

Makes 3 gallons.

NONA'S DOWNTOWN MARKET
Local Products in a New Urban Market
OWENSBORO

Owensboro's historic downtown is currently enjoying revitalization. Century-old and older brick buildings decorated with handsome architectural details are being converted to apartments, shops, and offices. In one of these buildings, located just a couple of blocks from the riverfront, you'll find a street level corner store that has a mission to bring the bounty of local farmers to the residents of the city.

"I'm blessed that they [the farmers] trust me with their stuff, " says Maria Kelly, owner of Nona's Downtown Market. Spend a few minutes with Kelly and you will trust her, too. Her passion for creating the perfect customer experience is evident in every detail of this inviting emporium.

The first sights that greet customers after they walk through the doors are displays of colorful vegetables, flowers, and fruits. Natural light pouring in from tall Palladian windows makes their colors pop. The produce is so enticing that even children, not generally vegetable lovers, are drawn to the baskets of multi-colored potatoes, peppers, squash, chilies, tomatoes, and onions. Other baskets contain fresh fruits, such as apples, blueberries (in season) and citrus.

Kelly and her staff, which includes her daughter Lataysha, cheerfully spend time with each customer who has a question or is seeking advice about a particular product or ingredient.

Originally from Boston, Kelly always enjoyed the "little shops with fresh, local products" she knew in that city. Her husband is from Owensboro, so they eventually wound up here because they thought it would be "a great place to raise our family."

Kelly's family ties echo through the store. "Nona," its namesake, was her grandmother Ella Lena. Her picture hangs on one corner of the market, as does a photograph of Kelly's mother.

Make your way past the colorful produce carts and you'll quickly come upon a maze of handmade and artisanal products including locally made soaps, candles, baskets, and pottery. A refrigerator and freezer case contains JD Country Milk (see p. 164), local cheeses, beef, goat meat, poultry, and fresh eggs.

Nona's Downtown Market
126 West Second Street
Owensboro, KY 42303
(270) 926-8183
www.nonasowensboro.com

Monday - Friday:
 9 a.m. - 6 p.m.
Saturday:
 9 a.m. - 5 p.m.

Ice cream lovers should pay special attention to the selection of pints from Meltdown of Bowling Green. Unusual and mouth filling flavors such as Bourbon Peach Tea Sorbet or Concord Crush are made with Kentucky grown ingredients.

For customers needing ideas about how to use the cornucopia of ingredients offered her, Kelly has thoughtfully provided a "cookbook nook." You are invited to browse through the shelf of cookbooks for recipes and cooking tips.

Three other businesses reside inside the market. **Creative RU** has a couple of tables where customers can paint their own pottery and, in season, fashion Christmas tree ornaments. **Petal & Pine** is an Owensboro florist that supplies fresh bouquets and floral arrangements to the market.

Wheatgrass Juice Bar and Kitchen Store serves up a variety smoothies and health drinks, the most inspiring of which may be the bright green Incredible Hulk blended from kale, spinach, wheatgrass, apple, banana, pineapple, mango, and coconut milk. It's packed with A, C, and K vitamins.

Wheatgrass owner Shauna Jones perfectly sums up the community spirit so evident at Nona's, "It's a great place to get your business started. All the vendors are working together. It just synergized."

OLD HICKORY BAR-B-Q
Six Generations of Serving Mutton "Q"
OWENSBORO

In addition to the difficulty of finding a parking space in the restaurant's lot, one of the first things you'll notice about Old Hickory is the enormous stack of eponymous logs stacked next to the restaurant's pit room and smokehouse. The pit masters here are loading their fireboxes with the wood to flavor mutton, chicken, beef brisket, pork (ribs and Boston butt), hams, and turkey breasts. It's a round-the-clock operation, since the meat goes on the grill one morning and is slowly cooked and smoked until it comes off the grills 24 hours later and the whole process is repeated.

Old Hickory traces its root to 1918, when Charles Forman started cooking and serving mutton. This is the restaurant that the locals recommend and bring their guests to when they want to show off Owensboro's famous barbecue.

The sixth generation of Forman's family still runs Old Hickory today.

Its history, as well as that of the city, is documented in a display of mostly black and white photographs in the entry alcove. A large world map on one wall bristles with pins showing the hometowns of people who have eaten here. Every state is represented, as well as countries in Europe, Asia, South America, Australia,

174

Old Hickory Bar-B-Q
338 Washington Avenue
Owensboro, KY 42301
(270) 926-9000
www.oldhickorybbqky.com

Sunday - Thursday:
  9 a.m. - 9 p.m.
Friday - Saturday:
  9 a.m. - 10 p.m.

and sub-Saharan Africa. A framed proclamation on the wall near the door dated May 7, 2010 from Governor Steven Beshear, names burgoo the Official State Dish. Very appropriate, since Hickory Pit's thick and savory version, made with mutton, chicken, and pork, is the perfect introduction to this Kentucky specialty.

The best way to sample the smoky goodness from the pit is by ordering one of the Combination Plates. You can chose three meats and two sides. Sliced beef brisket is meltingly tender. Pulled pork and chicken have the perfect degree of smoke flavor. Mutton is served sliced, chopped (and mingled with tangy barbecue sauce, which makes an outstanding sandwich), and as mutton ribs.

These ribs are not for mutton neophytes. They will probably be too gamy. But mutton connoisseurs will want to gnaw every scrap of the fatty meat from the bones.

Barbecued baked beans, mashed potatoes and gravy, and crisp onion rings are among the sides that complement the "Q."

A variety of pies and cobblers grace the dessert menu, but locals also swear by the big bowls of luscious banana pudding, topped with the perfect proportion of vanilla wafers and whipped cream. But do know there's no alcohol served here. Soft drinks only.

While every thing is available for carry out, do take the time to enjoy your meal in one of the homey dining rooms. The older part of the restaurant has a stone fireplace. The music playing in the background is exactly what you'd expect in a restaurant in Owensboro, hometown of Bill Monroe and the International Bluegrass Museum, www.bluegrass-museum.org.

BLUEBERRIES OF DAVIESS COUNTY
A Dozen Blueberry Varieties
UTICA

As you travel south, away from Owensboro's riverfront and head along the main thoroughfare of Frederica Street, the historic district gives way to an Anywhere America four-lane highway of shopping malls and fast food outlets. But instead of then yielding to mile after mile of suburbia, in just a few miles (and a few minutes) Frederica changes into Highway 431 and the road is bounded on both sides by acres and acres of flat farm interrupted by occasional, unexpected rises in the land.

A large brick building, Southern Oaks Elementary School, looms at the intersection of 431 and Hill Bridge Road. Turn left down Hill Bridge and wind through the (mostly) flat fields planted in corn and soybeans. There are a couple of hills, a few turns, and then, on the left, there's a blue-painted iron sign with the word "BLUEBERRIES" spelled out in the metal. You have reached Blueberries of Daviess County.

Total travel time from downtown Owensboro was about 15 minutes.

Royce and Nancy McCormick started growing blueberries in 2001 when tobacco was declining. Three acres of their farm are devoted to about 2500 blueberry bushes comprised of 12 different varieties. The reason for the different types is to extend the growing season. Each ripens at a different time starting in early June and continuing into late July.

Alternating with the rows of bushes are rows of metal poles topped with white crosspieces. They are strung with wires supporting fine white netting that lets in sunlight, but keeps birds from eating the whole crop before humans can get to it.

Visitors are welcome to stop by the farm during growing season to purchase already picked berries or to wander through the bushes and pick their own.

Blueberries of Daviess County
1401 Hill Bridge Road
Utica, KY 42376
(270) 926-6510
www.blueberriesofdaviesscounty.com

June and July
 Monday, Wednesday, Friday,
 Saturday:
  8 a.m. - 5 p.m.

Blueberry Key-Lime Pie

⅓ c. Lime Juice
2 egg yolks
1 can condensed milk
1 graham cracker pie crust
½ c. blueberries

• Combine juice, yolks and milk. Stir until smooth.
• Pour into pie crust.
• Drop blueberries into pie.
• Bake 350 degrees F. for 15-20 minutes. Let cool. Refrigerate.

DAVE'S STICKY PIG
Outstanding Dry-Rubbed Ribs

MADISONVILLE

Dave's Sticky Pig is conveniently located on the outskirts of Madisonville, just a couple of minutes west from Exit 42 of the Pennyrile Parkway. But that doesn't necessarily make it easy to find. Turn off of Hwy. 70 into the Madison Square Shopping Center and don't be fooled into looking for Dave's among the main stores. It's in a former Baskin-Robbins shop in an out lot in front of the shopping center's parking lot. Look for the smoke from the pit out back and the sign in the front featuring a pink pig sitting by a log fire.

This a tiny operation compared to the barbecue giants of Owensboro. With only a few tables, most of the business is carry-out. So if you want to eat in, try to go off peak lunch or dinner hours. All of the meat is smoked and cooked using wood only (hickory and oak) and it's all cooked "low and slow." Owner and pit master Dave Webb uses different combinations of spice rubs for each of his different meats – pork shoulder, pork ribs, chicken, ham, and beef brisket. Mix-and-match ingredients include ancho chili powder, cumin, allspice, mustard, and paprika.

Since this is Western Kentucky, mutton is on the menu, too, but not all the time. So call ahead to find out about availability.

All of the meat is notably smoky, tender, and flavorful. None is sauced when it is served, but half a dozen house made barbecue sauces are available. Each is inspired by the style of the great barbecue regions such as Georgia, Memphis, or Texas. The Sticky Pig Sauce is made with beer and described as sort of a Goldilocks of sauces, "tart and spicy without being too hot or too sweet."

That said, feel free to ignore them all, since the spices and the smoke make the meat just right on its own!

Dave's Sticky Pig
206 Madison Square Drive
Madisonville, KY 42431
(270) 326-5100
www.davesstickypig.com

Monday - Thursday:
  11 .m. - 8 p.m.
Friday - Saturday:
  11 a.m. - 9 p.m.
Sunday:
  11 a.m. - 5 p.m.

The pork ribs, for example, may spoil you for any other pork ribs *anywhere*. Period. They are smoked right through to the bones and the spice combination is exactly right, enhancing the meat without getting in the way of its essential flavor. Any sauce would tip the flavor balance away from this piggy perfection.

Equal care is taken with the sides. Do know that the Sticky Pig slaw and potato salad is vinegar-, rather than mayonnaise-based. But the go-to side is most surely the very smoky baked beans, which are sweet without being cloying. (Maple syrup is among the ingredients.) They are also seasoned with pork or brisket, with flavorful bark on, so hence the smoke character.

Speaking of balance, something sweet (but not too sweet) is a welcome palate cleanser after a satisfying plate of Dave's savory, smoky meat. And Dave Webb provides an excellent option with his homemade bread pudding. Dense and sweet, it tickles the tongue with hints of vanilla and sweet spices.

Dave's Sticky Pig's Banana Pudding
Reprinted from The Kentucky Barbecue Book *by Wes Berry.*

2 ½ c. sugar
2 ½ c. whole milk
½ c. sifted cornstarch
4 eggs
1 oz. sifted flour
⅛ t. cinnamon
¼ t. nutmeg
1 oz. butter
1 oz. real vanilla extract
5 medium bananas, sliced
1 T. lemon juice
1 (13.3 oz.) bag vanilla wafers

• Use fully ripe bananas and refrigerate them before slicing to help them hold their shape. Slice into ¼ inch slices and toss with lemon juice to coat completely. Refrigerate. Drain lemon juice before using in the pudding.
• Make a double boiler by fitting a smaller saucepan snuggly inside a large one. Place water in the large saucepan and set stove to medium-high heat. You will have to add water to the larger saucepan a few times during the cooking process.
• In a saucepan, combine milk with sugar and cornstarch. Stir occasionally until sugar is fully dissolved and the custard seems to thicken slightly, about 20 minutes.
• Measure the flour, cinnamon, and nutmeg into a sifter. Sifting these three items together before adding them to the milk helps mix them.
• Using a whisk, lightly beat eggs in a mixing bowl. Temper the eggs with about a cup of the hot custard by stirring them briskly with a whisk while slowly pouring the custard into them. The outside of the bowl should be warm to the touch before you add the contents to the saucepan of custard. Add the eggs. Then add sifted cinnamon, nutmeg, and flour to the custard pot and cook about 30 to 45 more minutes in the double boiler, stirring occasionally. The custard will really thicken up as it cooks. When it seems as thick as it's going to get, remove from heat and add vanilla and butter.
• Pour a layer of pudding mixture in the bottom of a casserole dish large enough to hold the wet ingredients; add a layer of whole vanilla wafers, followed by a layer of half of the bananas. Repeat as many times as necessary to use up all the ingredients. Top with crumbled vanilla wafers.

179

GOLDEN GLAZE BAKERY & DELI
Delicious Doughnuts — And Holes
MADISONVILLE

Among the health-conscious, there are plenty of "power breakfasts," from granola and fresh fruit to wheat toast and vegetable-laden omelets. But sometimes there is simply nothing better for breakfast than fresh doughnuts.

Fluffy rings of yeasty dough, preferably hot from the fryer and sweet with a thin, crisp sugar glaze, are just perfect with a hot, black mug of coffee. And no doughnuts are fresher than those found at Golden Glaze.

Do not be put off by the plain beige wooden building with brown trim and a minimalist sign that simply identifies it as "Golden Glaze." Inside is a display counter stocked with trays of sweet goodies. These include cake doughnuts, Long Johns, jelly doughnuts, cinnamon 8's, apple fritters, glazed or iced sugar cookies, and plain, chocolate, blueberry or caramel-topped glazed doughnuts.

Mike Powers has owned the bakery since 1998, though he worked there as an employee before that. All doughnuts and cookies are made fresh daily. All are made by hand. None is ever frozen or sold the next day. (Powers gives away what hasn't sold by the end of the day to nursing homes and other places that can use them.)

He and his small staff (most of whom are members of his family) are up in the very wee hours of the morning every day but Sunday mixing dough and cutting out pastries by hand.

"Glazed doughnuts are a yeast product and need time to rise," he explains. This fermentation time is sensitive to temperature and barometric pressure, so Powers says he can tell the weather by how long it takes to bake his products in the morning.

The attention to detail is evident in the signature glazed doughnuts. First, they are about 50 percent larger that the average boxed doughnut. But they also seem about 50 percent lighter. As the name of the shop declares, they are indeed a light golden color and every surface, including inside the holes, has been hand-painted

Golden Glaze Bakery & Deli
67 North Franklin Street
Madisonville, KY 42431
(270) 821-7144
www.goldenglaze.net

Monday - Friday:
  5 a.m. - 4 p.m.
Saturday:
  5 a.m. - 12 p.m.

with a tissue-thin sugar glaze. Each sweet bite really does melt in the mouth.

The most popular items, the ones that sell out every day without fail, are the doughnut holes. They are the exception to Golden Glaze's 10 percent discount on buying 10 dozen or more doughnuts.

"Sometimes I think I should open a doughnut hole shop," muses Powers.

*K*entucky has a remarkable state parks' system of 59 parks and historic sites. The ones designated "resort parks" have lodges and cottages where visitors can stay overnight and enjoy a host of activities, from hiking and fishing to more sedate pastimes such as card tournaments and folk music concerts.

One of the state's most beautiful, and most peaceful, resort parks is Pennyrile Forest State Resort Park near Dawson Springs. It's an excellent "base of operations" for exploring the food finds of Western Kentucky.

Traveling between the towns in this book on the hunt for barbecue, country ham, and more, most of the landscape on either side of the roads and highways will be rolling or flat farmland. This small, 863-acre park is actually tucked away inside the 15,331-acre Pennyrile State Forest, offering a wooded oasis to rest and recuperate after a busy day of tracking down the region's best foodstuffs.

The unusual name is derived from "pennyroyal." American Pennyroyal is a wildflower native to this region belonging to the mint family. Growing to about a foot in height, characteristically in large, aromatic patches, the stalk is long and slender. Its tiny pale blue flowers bloom all along these stalks in late summer. When settlers first arrived in the region in the 1800s, it was abundant and this part of the state became known, with the locals' inflection, as the Pennyrile.

Most of the flower's habitat has now been converted to agriculture. But it still blooms along the Pennyrile Trail within the park.

The 24-room stone lodge looks like it was picked up from Bavaria and plunked down in this Western Ken-

**Pennyrile Forest
State Resort Park**
20781 Pennyrile Lodge Road
Dawson Springs, KY 42408
(270) 797-3421
www.parks.ky.gov/parks/
resortparks/pennyrile-forest

tucky woods. A large lobby fireplace blazes in wintertime and the lodge dining room overlooks a 56-acre lake. Recreation includes an 18-hole golf course, as well as nine intersecting hiking trails.

Frankly, state park food has a long way to go before it can be recommended as part of a culinary tour. (State Parks' officials know this and maintain they are working on upgrades.) Do know that occasional game dinners, held when state elk and bison herds are culled, are actually pretty darned good.

Nonetheless, consider staying in one of the dozen cottages, eight of which overlook the lake. Each contains a fully equipped kitchen, so you can bring area delicacies home and prepare for dinner.

The best cottage may be Number 508, also known as the Honeymoon Cottage. It has a spiral staircase leading to a sleeping loft with a double bed and a little window at the head of the bed overlooking treetops.

There are three other resort parks in the region, though each is much bigger than Pennyrile. They are Lake Barkley State Resort Park (Cadiz), Kenlake State Resort Park (Hardin), and Kentucky Dam Village State Resort Park (Gilbertsville). All have both lodge rooms and cottages.

For more information about all of Kentucky's State Parks, go to http://www.parks.ky.gov.

MEACHAM COUNTRY HAMS
Country Ham in the Countryside
STURGIS

To appreciate the geography of the Western Kentucky country ham tradition, take time to travel to Sturgis in Union County. That's where you'll travel south on U.S. Highway 60 from Henderson, through farming country very near the Ohio River border with Illinois, to the Meacham family farmstead.

Once you turn off the main highway, venture along O'Nan Dyer Road to Meacham's Country Ham. A sign on the left marks the farm road lined on either side by acres of corn. This leads to the homestead and retail shop.

Pull into the gravel parking lot behind the white frame farmhouse, parts of which date from 1860. If you happen to be here from late May to mid-September, the sounds of a Kentucky summer are all you will hear when you open the car door. Insects buzz. There

may be the occasional "scree-scree" of a hawk. Unless there's some wind, there are no other sounds at all.

The Meacham's tradition of curing hams stretches back to 1932. That's when William Meacham, grandfather of current owner Amanda Meacham Coy, started the business. But the family tradition is even longer. Meacham learned how to cure hams from his grandmother.

Coy explains that her family's curing recipe "is not as salty as some and there's a little sweet, too." A deep red color to the meat is a result of the smoking process. While there is a retail store on the premises, as well as a curing house, most of the firm's business, about 85 percent, is online.

Hams have been shipped to all 50 states as well as overseas. Restaurants that serve Meacham's Ham include The Cannibal, a meat-focused gastro-pub in

Meacham Country Hams
705 O'Nan Dyer Road
Sturgis, KY 42459
(800) 552-3190
www.meachamhams.com

Winter
 Monday - Friday:
  8 a.m. - 3 p.m.

*E-mail for summer hours at info@
 meachamhams.com.*

New York City and, closer to home, at the Beaumont Inn in Harrodsburg (p. 38), and the Garage Bar in Louisville (p. 74).

Coy says her number one seller is Derby Style, a ham not aged as long as traditional country hams, so it's a little milder. It, like the original Meacham's ham, is available as a whole or half boneless ham, as well as in packages of eight-ounce slices.

Other products include thicker six-ounce breakfast slices, two ounce biscuit slices, and pepper-rubbed ham. Get ground country ham to mix with pickle and mayonnaise to make an excellent spread to serve on beaten biscuits. Original, pepper, maple, and applewood-smoked bacon, as well as smoked country sausage are sold here, too.

Authentic Red-Eye Gravy

The starting point for this most traditional of Southern breakfast gravies will be the pan drippings from frying the Meacham's breakfast slices of country ham. Spoon it over the ham and its proper accompaniment, grits.

From the brochure available at the Meacham's Store.

- To make a good red-eye gravy, add cold water to drippings from ham at 2-3 times the amount of drippings.
- Add black coffee to taste and color.
- Bring to a rapid boil for about 1 minute.
- Add more water or sugar to taste.

FERRELL'S HAMBURGERS
A Local Institution
HOPKINSVILLE

opkinsville's most important historic site is the Trail of Tears Commemorative Park. In the late 1830s, the U.S. Government ordered the forced relocation of the Cherokee people from their home in the Carolinas to reservations in Oklahoma. The park is situated on land known to be one of the campgrounds used on the long relocation route known as the Trail of Tears. Two Cherokee chiefs who died during the journey, Fly Smith and White Path, are buried here. The park, with its museum, is an excellent reason to visit the seat of Christian County. While you are there, take a culinary journey back in time and eat at Ferrell's Hamburgers.

Look for the funny little brick building with green tile awnings and a big green, white, and red neon sign, perched on a street corner in the middle of downtown. When you step through the door, you'll step back to 1929, the year Ferrell's opened. Very little has changed.

The walls of the tiny interior are made of bright green and white tile blocks. Seven green stools are lined up at the lunch counter, behind which three employees manage to wedge themselves into a narrow space where they grill burgers, dispense soft drinks,

and answer the phone for carryout orders. A large round electric clock bordered with green neon letters spelling out "Ferrell's, Since 1929" is perched high on a shelf in one corner. An ancient wooden cash register with keyed levers onto which prices are punched sits in a custom-built niche in the back wall's metal shelving.

By no stretch of the imagination is a Ferrell's hamburger "gourmet." What it is is authentically good. When you sidle onto a stool and place your order, the woman at the griddle (It *will* be a woman and she will be wearing a hair net.) takes a chunk of ground beef

Ferrell's Hamburgers
1001 South Main Street
Hopkinsville, KY 42240
(270) 886-1445
www.facebook.com/pages/
  Ferrells-Hamburgers-of-
  Hopkinsville/324131284319610

Open 24 hours.

the size and shape of a racquetball out of a refrigerator under the counter and puts it on the hot fry grill, where she proceeds to flatten it with a broad metal spatula into a disc.

The meat sizzles for about five minutes per side as she turns and tends it, making sure it cooks evenly.

When the burger is done (no rare, medium rare, or other degrees of doneness other than "done" here), she reaches for a bag of white Rainbo bread buns, takes one out of the plastic, opens it to add chopped raw onions from one bowl on the counter and sliced pickles from another. Ketchup and mustard are optional.

The assembled hamburger is wrapped in paper and handed to you. Since you are going to unwrap it immediately in order to eat it, this seems unnecessary, but there are no plates, not even paper, so this is how it's done.

The grilled-to-order burger is piping hot, with wonderful crispy edges from its time on the hot metal surface. It is perfect. Bagged chips are available. Coke products are canned, but you can get a cup of ice.

Ferrell's also serves hot dogs and chili and there's a "Special Breakfast" of ham, sausage, or bacon with two eggs, toast and coffee. But the Ferrell's fame deservedly comes from these great little hamburgers.

By the way, there are two other Ferrell's locations. Find the one in Madisonville is at 112 N. Main St., just around the corner from Golden Glaze Bakery (see p. 180). The other one is in Cadiz at 2021 Main St.

NEWSOM'S OLD MILL STORE
Col. Newsom's Award-Winning Country Ham
PRINCETON

*P*rinceton has a handsome Main Street lined with rows of 19th century brick buildings housing shops and offices. It's easy to imagine that the street looked much like this when the town's signature historic event, the attack by the vigilante group known as the Night Riders, took place on December 1, 1906. That's when they raided the town and burned down the world's largest tobacco warehouses to protest a monopoly that was leaving local farmers in debt.

The only raiders in evidence in Princeton today are the legions of country ham devotees who make pilgrimages to Newsom's Old Mill Store at the corner of Main and Hawthorne Streets. Look for the red and white striped awnings. The sign over the door reads, "Vintage 1880. Take a Walk Thru the Past."

But that gives little indication of the treasure to be found inside.

The interior may also distract from the ham seeker's goal. The creaky wooden floors are piled with stacks of edible goods, from jar after jar of jams, jellies, sauces, sorghum, and other preserves to bottles of vintage soft drinks. Baskets of hard candy in a dazzling array of flavors are stacked on flats made out of upside-down antique wooden Coca-Cola boxes.

You may have heard of apple butter, but what about pumpkin butter or sweet potato pecan butter? Not only are there strawberry preserves, but strawberry-rhubarb preserves, too. A true Southern delicacy, pickled watermelon rind, is sold here. If you've been having trouble finding pickled quails eggs for that special recipe, look no farther. Newsom's has them.

But once you make your way through this maze of sweets you'll find the meat counter at the back of the store. Savory is really why you've come, because this is the source for Col. Newsom's Aged Kentucky Country Hams.

The Newsom of the name was the late William Newsom who started curing hams to sell at the store his father, H. C. Newsom, had founded in 1917, a couple of doors down from the current retail space.

In the 1970s, famed chef and cookbook author James Beard discovered

Newsom's Old Mill Store
208 East Main Street
Princeton, KY 42445
(270) 365-2482
www.newsomscountryham.com

Monday - Friday:
 9 a.m. - 4:30 p.m.
Saturday:
 9 a.m. - 3 p.m.

Newsom's special salt and brown sugar cured, natural climate-aged hams. He gave cooking demonstrations with it and many Americans rediscovered the complex flavor of country ham that most Kentuckians had never forgotten.

William Newsom's daughter, Nancy Newsom Mahaffey, heads the business today. The self-styled "Ham Lady" Mahaffey learned curing techniques from her father and has guided Newsom's to even more culinary fame.

She was invited to take her hams to the World Congress of Dry Cured Hams in Aracena, Spain in 2009. It was the only invitation to an American. The meat made such an impression that one of the hams is now on display in the city's Jamon Museum.

Probably the reason for this honor is the uniqueness of one of Mahaffey's products. She cures and sells a prosciutto-style ham, more expensive than her traditional aged country hams (also available as a free-range product), and served in delectable, tissue thin slices, as befits this style.

Hams (whole and half), sliced ham by the pound, bacon, and sausage are sold at the counter. But you can also get a made-to-order sandwich. There are no tables where you can eat it, but customers have been known to enjoy a country ham sandwich while sitting on the stone wall in front of the store.

Newsom's Center or End Slice Aged Country Ham

A lot of country ham is sold in pre-cooked slices. But here's the perfect way, as recommended by Newsom's, to prepare uncooked ham.

- Trim off the hard outer edge of meat and remove rind. DO NOT TRIM FAT. (This adds flavor, and no other fat will be needed.)
- Fry in large heavy skillet, turning lean away from the hottest point of the skillet.
- FRY SLOWLY. Do not over fry. (This will make the ham hard, dry and tough.) Turn slices often. Ham is usually done when fat is transparent and beginning to brown.
- For milder or LESS SALTY taste, soak slices in lukewarm water or sweet milk for up to 30 minutes before frying. (For frying ham slices with extremely red, rosy color, which are more aged, less frying time will be required.)

189

BROADBENT'S GOURMET MARKET & DELI
Award-Winning Country Ham & More
KUTTAWA

*A*s you stand in front of the lunch counter in the Broadbent's Deli where customers place orders for sandwiches, look to your right. You'll see a corridor wall lined with award ribbons – about 15 feet of them – for Broadbent's country hams. Since 1967, the hams from the company founded in 1963 by Smith Broadbent, Jr. and by now owned by Ronny and Beth Drennan, have won an impressive 16 Grand Champion titles at the Kentucky State Fair, more than any other producer.

Besides their all-around excellence, what's notable about any state fair winning hams is that they are auctioned to raise money for charity. In August 2014, the Broadbent ham fetched a whopping, and record-setting, $2 million, which, for a ten-pound ham, works out to $200,000 per pound. That's good news for the beneficiaries. The very good news for consumers is that Broadbent's estimable ham sells for less than one ten-thousandths of that price, at just under $20 per pound.

In contrast to the farm setting of Meacham's

and the country storefront of Newsom's, Broadbent's is housed in a modern 20,000 square-foot processing facility behind a truck stop just a few hundred feet from Exit 40 off Interstate 24.

The spotless processing plant is so large that Broadbent's cures hams for other producers, as well as their own. But that doesn't mean that all the hams taste the same.

The Broadbent hams spend a full nine months on premises. These include four months in the aging room. According to owner Ronny Drennan, "By USDA rules, a country ham has to lose 18 percent of

Broadbent's Gourmet Market & Deli
257 Mary Blue Road
Kuttawa, KY 42055
(800) 841-2202
www.broadbenthams.com

Monday - Friday:
 8 a.m. - 4 p.m.
Saturday:
 9 a.m. - 4 p.m.

its weight. But our hams lose 25 to 30 percent, so they have a different texture and flavor than hams cured quicker."

Even though the facility is enormous, the market at the front is made inviting by cheerful pale yellow walls, and yellow and red linoleum block floors. After a lunch of a country ham or bacon sandwich (Chicken salad is on the menu, too, but really, go for the pork!) customers can browse the cases for a variety of Broadbent's meats. Center steaks, biscuit slices, bacon, sausage, and hock and ham pieces for soup flavoring are some of the products. A variety of kitchen utensils and gift items are for sale, too.

By the way, 2014 was an exceptionally good year for Broadbent's. Not only did its ham set the charity auction record at the Kentucky State Fair, it also took home the National Championship Country Ham Award in the Uncooked Country Ham category. Some pig!

Green Eggs and Ham

Not just found amongst the pages of Dr. Seuss. This comes from Broadbent's website. It's a great variation on devilled eggs and makes an eye-catching hors d'oeuvre.

6 slices Broadbent's sliced cooked country ham, chopped
12 large hard-cooked eggs
1 ripe avocado, peeled and mashed
2 T. finely chopped onion
1 clove garlic, minced
2 T. mayonnaise
1 ½ T. fresh lime juice
1 t. hot sauce
1 small tomato, peeled, seeded, and finely chopped

• Cut eggs lengthwise and carefully remove yolks. Mash yolks with a fork; add avocado and next 5 ingredients, stirring well.
• Fold in tomato, and spoon into egg whites.
• Top with ham. Can use Broadbent's ground ham in place of chopped ham.

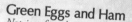

CATFISH KITCHEN
Fried Catfish & Fixings
BENTON

remarkable statistic about the geography of Kentucky is that there are more miles of running water – rivers, streams, and creeks – within its borders than in any other of the lower 48 states. Only Alaska, which of course is many times larger, has more flowing water. This means that Kentucky has an impressive fish fauna, including several species of catfish. Among the best kind for eating is the Channel Catfish, which is abundant in the Cumberland and Tennessee Rivers of Western Kentucky.

For that reason, fried catfish is a traditional favorite in this part of the state. One of the best places to enjoy it is the Catfish Kitchen, owned by Wes and Judy Davis.

The lakeside restaurant is located just off Highway 641 about 15 minutes south of Kentucky Dam Village State Resort Park. Know that the address is a little confusing. Officially it's Benton, but if you are coming from the Purchase Parkway, rather than from the state park, the restaurant is just outside of Draffenville.

If you don't want to wait for a table, arrive just as the restaurant opens. Even with that, cars will already be streaming into the parking lot. The waiting area, lined with wooden benches, and decorated with a hodge-podge of objects ranging from old metal soft drinks signs to a stuffed brown bear, quickly fills with patrons.

As soon as the doors to the L-shaped dining room open, the wooden tables and chairs fill up and no one has to wait for a first bite. Bowls of white beans, creamy slaw, and hush puppies are already on the tables. These are included in the price of catfish, chicken, shrimp, fried clam, and frog legs dinners. All

Catfish Kitchen
136 Teal Run Circle
Benton KY 42025
(270) 362-7306
www.facebook.com/
CatfishKitchen

Wednesday - Saturday:
 4 p.m. - 9 p.m.
Saturday:
 11 a.m. - 9 p.m.

Closed in January.

of which are less than $15. Seniors and children's meals are considerably less.

Portions are generous. The catfish dinner contains two large, cornmeal-breaded fillets; the fish has a delicate, sweet flavor. Wes Davis candidly explains that his fish are farm-raised in Alabama, not taken from the muddy depths of the nearby rivers. But the cornmeal coating is absolutely traditional, and addictive.

The Davises bought the restaurant more than a quarter century ago. At one time the lake overlooked by the dining room windows was a pay fishing lake and is now home to a fish population that is fed the restaurant's leftover hush puppies. It's a pretty setting and coupled with the delicious, very reasonably priced fare, is certainly why the Catfish Kitchen is so popular.

Judy Davis confirms this popularity. "We serve several hundred [customers] a night on Fridays and Saturdays. We're small, but we're busy!"

HITCHING POST &
OLD COUNTRY STORE
Vintage Soda Pop Collection & Tastings
AURORA

urora is best known as the location of Kenlake State Resort Park. It's located in dry Marshall County. But just because no alcohol is sold or served doesn't mean that visitors will be thirsty. For a fascinating tour through the world of soda pop, stop by the Hitching Post & Old Country Store, only two miles from the park.

The two stores are housed in adjacent log buildings that are much bigger in size than they look from the road.

Proprietor Su Festen, who migrated from the Chicago area to Western Kentucky, has assembled an impressive collection of some 180 different sodas from around the country, which are found in the Old Country Store side of the complex. She'll walk you through the labels with the expertise of a soft drinks sommelier. If you've wondered what sarsaparilla, real cream soda, or birch beer tastes like, wonder no more. There are several examples. Festen holds weekly soft drinks tastings of ten select sodas at a time and you can even buy a souvenir tasting glass for $4.95 in which to savor the samples.

While adults might favor the drier or citrus-flavored sodas, kids are all about the sweet, fruity ones. Among their favorites, says Festen, are the "totally gross flavors" made by Avery's of New Britain, Connecticut. What 10-year-old wouldn't be enticed by a bottle of purple Monster

Mucus (strawberry and blue raspberry), yellow Kitty Piddle (pineapple and orange), or foggy white Dog Drool (orange or lemon)?

As eye-catching as the shelves lined with colorful bottles are, that's just part of the nostalgic fun to be found here. The store is stocked with old-fashioned candies, such as Necco Wafers and even candy cigarettes. (When was the last time you saw *those*?) An assortment of bite-sized, paper-wrapped salt-water taffy flavors is sold by the pound. (Check out the antique scale used for weighing it.) And the room smells enticingly of different kinds of flavored roast coffee beans. Several varieties of tea are found here, too.

Both the sodas and the candies harken back to a pre-digital childhood and Festen sells a selection of completely battery-and-button free toys and games to accompany them. There are marbles, tiddlywinks,

**Hitching Post &
Old Country Store**
16474 U.S. Highway 68 East
Aurora, KY 42048
(270) 474-2266
www.hitchingpost.us

Memorial Day - Labor Day
 Tuesday - Saturday:
  9 a.m. - 6 p.m.
 Sunday:
  10 a.m. - 4 p.m.

Call for other seasonal hours.

slide whistles, pop guns, dominoes, and a magnetic fishing game, to name a very few.

The Hitching Post side caters to customers' sweet teeth, too. It features cases stocked with some 50 different flavors of fudge, though only about 18 are on display at any given time. All are homemade with real cane sugar and real butter.

The store is stocked with clothing, costume jewelry, and a variety of down-home decorative items. The room behind the Old Country Store is filled with antique furniture.

The high point of the Hitching Post's year is the annual Bubbles and Beans Festival, featuring soda pop tastings, a chili cook-off, and live music. It's held in September. Contact the store for the exact dates.

Susan with her cat, E.T.

Award-winning writer Susan Reigler, author of *Kentucky Bourbon Country: The Essential Travel Guide, The Complete Guide to Kentucky State Parks*, and co-author of *The Kentucky Bourbon Cocktail Book*, was born in Louisville the year Swaps won the Kentucky Derby. She holds a bachelor's degree in music from Indiana University and a master's degree in zoology from Oxford University, which she attended as a Humphrey Scholar. Currently, she is a lecturer and research associate in biology at Indiana University Southeast.

From 1992 to 2007, Reigler was a restaurant critic, beverage columnist and travel writer for the Louisville *Courier-Journal* and has been a judge for the James Beard Foundation Restaurant Awards since 1997. She also currently writes Kentucky restaurant reviews for the international travel and entertainment website, Gayot.com (pronounced "guy-oh").

Reigler serves on the board of directors of Bourbon Women (president as of 2015) and of Historic Locust Grove. She has conducted bourbon tastings from Seattle to Savannah and led tastings to benefit non-profit organizations including Locust Grove, The Falls of the Ohio Foundation, and Shaker Village at Pleasant Hill. She been a judge for more than a few bourbon cocktail contests and has helped many restaurants, retailers, and non-profit organizations select barrels from distilleries for private bourbon bottlings. She and co-author Joy Perrine host "Bourbon Cocktail Mixology" each year at The Kentucky Bourbon Festival. Reigler's next book, co-authored with bourbon historian Michael Veach, *The Kentucky Bourbon Tasting Notebook*, will be published in 2015.

MEET THE PHOTOGRAPHER

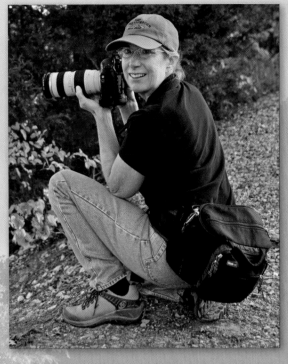

Pam Spaulding was a photojournalist for the *Louisville Courier-Journal* for 40 years.

Spaulding contributed to the photography that won the *Courier-Journal* and *Louisville Times* the 1976 Pulitzer Prize for coverage of court-ordered busing in Jefferson County, Kentucky. In 1984-85 she was a Nieman Fellow at Harvard University, only the seventh photographer to be selected since 1938.

Her primary work has been photographing the everyday lives of people in Kentucky but she also has taken every opportunity to pursue stories about Kentucky's flora and fauna. Since her retirement, she spends most of her time photographing birds.

She has had three books published of her work and has been published in numerous books and magazines such as *Horticulture*, the *National Geographic* and *Traveler* magazines.

Photo by Kenneth R. Weaver

ℱEATURED ℰSTABLISHMENTS

ℛECIPES

INDEX